Landy Publishing
1995

ISBN 1 872895 26 3

Landy Publishing have also published:

Accrington Observed by Brian Brindle & Bob Dobson
A Blackburn Miscellany edited by Bob Dobson
Policing in Lancashire by Bob Dobson
In Lancashire Language (Dialect Verse) edited by Bob Dobson
Concerning Clogs by Bob Dobson
Lancashire Limericks by John Sephton
Blackburn's West End by Matthew Cole
In Fine Fettle (Dialect Verse) by Peter Thornley & Michael May
Blackburn & Darwen A Century Ago by Alan Duckworth
Bits of Old Blackburn by Shaw, Hulme and Charles Haworth
The Annals of Trawden Forest by Fred Bannister

Details of these and all other Landy Publications may be obtained from Landy Publishing, 3 Staining Rise, Staining, Blackpool, FY3 0BU Tel/Fax 01253 886103. All books ordered from the publisher are sent post free to U.K. addresses.

PREFACE

The compiling of this book has been nothing more than a self-indulgence on my part. For some years I've wanted to compile a book to match *An Accrington Miscellany*, edited by John Goddard and compiled by Ronnie Digby and Alice Miller in 1970. In January 1994, I set out to achieve an ambition - to do something I would be proud of at the same time being seen as contributing to the written history of Accrington. Eighteen months later, having enjoyed every moment of research, I went to the printer. I'm pleased with the mixture, and I hope you are too. I know it is incomplete. For instance, there's nowt here about brickmaking or coalmining. I've missed out some tales that ought to be told. I've forgotten about certain people who deserve to be called *Accrington Achievers*. I could have prepared a book twice as thick and still have left something out. I've had to leave out some material which had been submitted to me for this book, and that has disappointed me. I hope someone will take up my challenge to "*get agate and do another like it*".

This book is a mixture (like fish, chips and peas). I've tried to place the material under headings even though sometimes they didn't quite fit, and anyway there's no particular order about the book. If no author is shown under a particular piece, I wrote it. Bear with me in the geography aspect - my definition of Accrington includes Huncoat, Church, Ossie, Clayton, Altham and Bash, even though some of those townships were previously outside the borough's boundaries.

I waste no opportunity of telling everyone that "*I was born and bred in Accrington - you can't **buy** class*." I hope this pride is reflected in my choice of material for the book.

Here I'd like to thank those people who have contributed to the book. I thank too the staff at Accrington Local History Library, especially Cath Duckworth, Helen Barrett, Josie Green and Heather Hizem. I thank Brian Ormerod for his line drawings; June Huntingdon, a new found cousin, for her never-failing help in sleuthing amongst old *Observers* and her ability to sniff out useful information; I thank my teachers at St. John's and the Grammar School for giving me something which stimulated my interest in local history, language and pride in my home town. I thank John Goddard and Frank Watson for always answering my questions on local topics and for keeping local history alive.

In the absence of my Grandma, Mum and Dad, and with my wife's approval, I dedicate this book to my aunt, Sally Watson, nee Dobson. No mother ever had a more caring daughter, no brother ever had a better sister than '*Eawr Sal*'. She has been a friend to many and a rock to which our family have anchored.

Bob Johnson

Autumn, 1995
"Acorns"
3, Staining Rise
Staining
Blackpool

3

'Tis opportune to look back upon olden times and contemplate our forefathers

Richard Ainsworth 1928

Contents

A.B.C.: ACCRINGTON'S BEER COMPANY

In common with most Lancashire towns, Accrington was a place where beer was brewed commercially. The man behind it was Nicholas Bentley, an industrious weaver who started a brewing company in 1868 close to where the *'Blockade Hotel'* now stands. As business improved, he bought land in Hood Street and put up two cottages, one of which was a brewhouse. In 1871, Thomas Thwaites, brother of Daniel, the Blackburn brewer, died, and Nicholas bought his newly erected brewery at Milnshaw.

Bentley's *'Milnshaw Brewery'* flourished. He and his sons bought and built houses and pubs. Nicholas died in 1888 aged 70, and his lads continued the family business. Sons Thomas and John were the active partners. In 1905, it was valued - properties, plant and goodwill - at £25,005.

In 1911, the directors were: Thomas (Blockade Hotel); John (Lytham); Sharples (37 Milnshaw Lane); James (27 Milnshaw Lane); Nicholas and Doctor (39 Milnshaw Lane). [Doctor was a common Christian name at that time.]

When son Sharples died, there was a family dispute over his shares, which he hadn't mentioned in his will. Were they, or the dividends from them, to go to his widow Caroline, or to his sons? He did stipulate that Caroline, to benefit from his will, had to live in Accrington. The matter went to Chancery Court in 1918.

In 1924, probably sickened by family disputing, the company was sold to John Smith's Tadcaster Brewery. The solicitor's bill came to £391-5s-7d and he generously wrote on it, *"say £390"*.

The properties included in the sale were:- The brewery: **The** *Blockade Hotel* (King Street): *New Brewery Inn* (Maudsley Street/Hood Street): *Railway Hotel* (Huncoat): *Junction Inn* (St. James Street/Paradise Street): Off-licence shop and houses in Milnshaw Lane: Properties in Cotton Street: *Cattle Market Inn* (King Street): *Borough Arms* (Oak Street): *Abbey Hotel* (Bank Street): *Spread Eagle* Beerhouse (Blackburn): *Bay Horse* Beerhouse (Colne): *Duke of Buccleugh* (Waterfoot): *George & Dragon* (Barrowford).

All was not harmony within the Bentley family. It was disclosed in Preston Police Court that the marriage of John and Matilda was not a happy one, and that they had parted. John had a *"lady friend"*, Cecily Higgins, and *"kept her"* in a house in Preston, where, one day in 1889, Matilda and her sister Grace Porritt visited them. They broke a window to get into the house, ransacked it and assaulted *"this other woman"*, who called herself Mrs. Sissy Bentley, with an umbrella. Fortunately for him, John was out. The sisters were summonsed for assaulting Sissy. What a performance it must have been. *"I'll dance on your grave"* was heard above the smashing of bottles. In court, it came out that the Bentleys had four good years together, then *"another woman"* came on the scene, followed by Sissy, a Burnley weaver. The magistrates weren't impressed with Sissy, or Bentley, and dismissed the case.

ACCRINGTON'S LICENSED HOUSES IN 1898

In 1898, the 84 beerhouses and fully licensed (i.e. spirits sold) hotels within the borough were re-assessed for rates. This resulted in them paying, collectively, another £500 to the town, or a third more than previously. The following list does not include registered clubs.

Lark Inn	Abbey Street	Crown Inn	Church Street
Curriers' Arms	ditto	Bridge Inn	ditto
Duke of Wellington	ditto	Borough Arms	Oak Street
Flying Dutchman	ditto	Beehive	Bank Street
Oak Tree Inn	ditto	Abbey Inn	ditto
Swan Hotel	ditto	Rising Sun	Cross Street
Hargreaves Arms	Manchester Road	Star Inn	Nuttall Street
Park Inn	ditto	Brittania	ditto
Tramway Inn	ditto	Derby Hotel	St. James Street
Weavers' Arms	Abbey Street	Junction	ditto
Red Lion	ditto	Lang's Arms	Dale Street
Black Horse	ditto	Richmond Hotel	Brown Street
Lord Nelson	Queen Street	Woodnook Inn	Woodnook
Old House at Home	Melbourne Street	Golden Cup	Union Street
Adelphi	Avenue Parade	New Market Tavern	ditto
Stanley Arms	Washington Street	Rosebud Inn	ditto
Cricketers' Arms	Barnes Street	Blockade Hotel	King Street
Queen's Hotel	Pitt Street	Horse Shoe Inn	School Street
King's Arms	Lee Street	Burns Inn	ditto
St. Leger	Plantation Street	Bull Hotel	King Street
Welcome Inn	Elephant Street	Palatine	Frederick Street
Pineapple	ditto	Slater's Arms	Whalley Road
Prince of Wales	Pitt Street	Hope and Anchor	ditto
Oddfellows	Blackburn Road	Castle Inn	ditto
Brown Cow	Bridge Street	Grey Horse	ditto
Commercial Hotel	Blackburn Road	Crown Inn	Dyke Nook
Bay Horse	Church Street	Australian Inn	Weir Street
Free Trade Inn	Blackburn Road	Model Inn	Milnshaw Lane
Globe	ditto	Royal Oak	Meadow Street
Royal Hotel	ditto	New Brewery	Maudsley Street
Antley Inn	ditto	St. John's Hotel	Arnold Street
Pickup's Arms	ditto	Great Eastern	ditto
Oak Tree	ditto	Peel's Arms	Burnley Road
Hyndburn Inn	ditto	Boar's Head	ditto
Spread Eagle	ditto	Peel Park Hotel	Peel Park
Cattle Market Inn	King Street	Victoria Hotel	Manchester Road
Imperial Hotel	Blackburn Road	Bay Horse	ditto
Crown Hotel	ditto	Dog and Partridge	Back Lane
Railway Hotel	ditto	Railway Hotel	Manchester Road
Thwaites Arms	ditto	Alma Inn	ditto
White Lion	Warner Street	Red Lion	Bedlam
Warner's Arms	ditto	Colliers' Arms	ditto

PUB PIECES

On the 26th June, 1899, the *'Railway Hotel'*, Blackburn Road was auctioned, along with its stables, coach houses, outbuildings and yard in Edgar Street. It was bought for £12,600. The *'Globe Inn'*, Blackburn Road, was built on land legally leased in 1853. On the 17th July, 1884, an auction took place at the *'Commercial Hotel'* of a brewery at 5, Sydney Street, along with houses, shop and stables in Manor Street. The brewery came with plant and machinery in good order, capable of brewing 6 loads per week, and with its own well with a good supply of water. Both lots were withdrawn through low bids. The *'Cemetery Hotel'*, Huncoat, changed its name from the *'Whittaker's Arms'* when the land across the road became a cemetery in 1864. On the 7th November, 1929, the *'Load of Mischief'* Hotel, Clayton was bought by Fred Newman from Fred Walmesley. The value of the stock was £417-6s-0d, the furnishings and effects were valued at £1,010-6s-8d, and the other values, less 16s-7d for broken windows, came to £1,552-10s-0d. The *'Bay Horse Hotel'*, probably Accrington's first hostelry, stood in Church Street, cheek-by-jowl with St. James' Church. Its licence was removed on the 18th December, 1920, after 169 years. A group of 25 tap room patrons presented Mr. & Mrs. Bill Mason, licencees for the previous six years, with an illuminated address for their kindness and courtesy.

❀ ❀ ❀ ❀ ❀ ❀

The following licenced houses had their licences refused by the Licencing Justices on the date or year shown in brackets:-

Pine Apple Inn (1906): *White Lion* (1906): *Lark Inn* (1906): *Beehive Inn* (1907): *Newmarket Tavern* (1908): *Colliers'Arms*, Bedlam (1908): *Prince of Wales Hotel* (1909): *Golden Cup* (1912): *Burns Inn* (1912): *New Model Inn* (1915): *Gardener's Arms* (1915): *Oddfellows' Home* (13th October, 1962): *Australian Inn* (31st July, 1964): *Navigation Inn*, Church (7th January, 1960): *Falcon Inn*, Ossie (11th June, 1959): *Borough Arms* (5th January, 1960): *Slater Arms* (7th January, 1938). This list is by no means exhaustive.

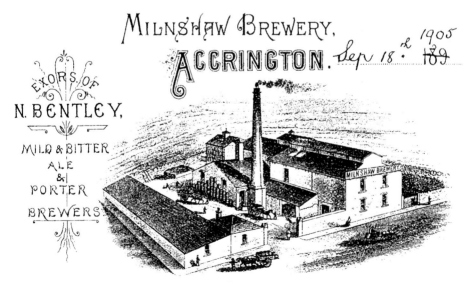

ACCRINGTON BOROUGH POLICE FORCE

A typical East Lancashire industrial town whose motto is *'Industry and Prudence Conquer'*, the borough of Accrington was incorporated in 1878, when the town was an inspector's station in the Blackburn Lower Division of the Lancashire Constabulary.

In the same year, however, the strong feeling invoked in the town by the Great Cotton Strike proved too much for the police to handle and the military were called in to assist in quelling the rioters and restoring the law. Such was the environment under which the Accrington Borough Police Force was formed in 1883.

Thirty-one officers, comprising one inspector, a detective sergeant, and 25 constables, were appointed under the command of Mr. Joseph Walker, who died the following year to be succeeded by James Beattie, a former county police officer at Accrington. Mr. Beattie's annual reports show that begging, assault, and drunkenness were the most prevalent offences of that period, and a great deal of trouble was experienced with the industrial population, for whom separate figures were shown in the reports. In 1886, the cost of policing the town's 32,000 residents is recorded to have been £2,961, but the effect of this policing can be seen by the reduction in the number of summonses issued between 1883 and the later years.

In 1929, Inspector George Sinclair succeeded Mr. Beattie and he was responsible for the change from the familiar oil lamp, carried on the centre buckle of the night constable's belt, to the 6lb. wet battery, which was recharged every day. Mr. Sinclair was followed by Mr. Holmes, who came to Accrington from Oldham. Like other Chief Constables, Mr. Holmes was also head of the fire brigade and ambulance services, for which he received the princely sum of £25 per annum for the extra responsibility. These services were carried out by members of the force, who received lessons in fire fighting in addition to their police training.

During Mr. Holmes' term of office, the town's excellent police offices, courts, and fire station were erected following the selection of the best of 12 entries in a nationally advertised competition. The foundation stone was laid in 1932 and despite a great controversy about the proposed use of Yorkshire facing stone in preference to the world famous Accrington brick, the buildings were formally opened on 9th May, 1935. Situated in what was then Sykes Street and now Spring Gardens, the new police station replaced the one in Marquis Street, now Broadway, which had a tunnel leading from it to the nearby Town Hall, where the courts were held.

On Mr. Holmes relinquishing his position as chief constable in 1936 to take up a similar post at Blackpool, he was succeeded by Mr. Charles H. Walters, who came from Worcester City Police and who was to leave in 1940 to take the post of chief constable of Lincoln. Those men who served under Mr. Walters knew that there was a set route to take on approaching and leaving the beats, even when the discretionary beat system and 18 police boxes were introduced in 1938. They wore the dog-collar style of tunic and a greatcoat, which was not to be taken out of use until the beginning of May each year.

In June, 1940, Mr. W. J. H. Palfrey came from Portsmouth to succeed Mr. Walters. An interesting paragraph from his annual report of 1942 reads, *"I think a great reduction in juvenile crime could be achieved if it were possible to deal with delinquent parents who are, in many instances, showing a complete lack of understanding and apathy towards their children".*

During the war, Mr. Palfrey served for a long period as Lieutenant Colonel in the British Control Commission in Europe. His deputy during his absence was Chief Inspector Nathan Todd, an 18-stone giant who made a great impression on the public of Accrington. Mr. Todd held the reins while the amalgamation arrangements were made but he retired before becoming a member of the Lancashire Constabulary. The two forces amalgamated in 1947.

An inventory prior to the merger revealed that the force had very little technical equipment and did not possess any storm or Tilley lamps, accident signs, or teleprinters. There was, however, the magnificent sum of £3,000 in the Widows Fund and a great spirit existed amongst the members of the force. In an effort to extend this spirit and assist relations between the Borough Force and the Constabulary, men from Accrington and the Church Division of the county force formed a cricket team which played in the local league.

At the time of amalgamation, the town's 12 beats were policed by 55 officers, assisted by 66 special constables. Of these 55 men, 38 did not elect to be transferred to other parts of the county, while Mr. Palfrey became a superintendent in the county force, and later its chief officer.

Cannon Street, Accrington.

Myers (Accrington) Limited
MARQUIS STREET MEWS,
ACCRINGTON.

A GRAVE TALE

Stephen Greenhalgh

'*Sellars Fold*' was the name of a group of cottages on the road to Hapton, half-a-mile past '*The Griffin*' pub. Even by 1905 standards, it was poor quality housing, but Esther Elizabeth Holden and her husband, William, lived there, poverty-stricken but happy. Because of their poverty and the damp conditions, Esther's health was poor. In January 1905, six months after bearing a child, Esther lay in bed, poorly and cold. William went for Dr. Shotton, who came from Hapton as soon as he could, to find her weak and "*clemmed*" (undernourished). He called again three days later. The house, like the weather, was bleak and bitter.

About 5am on the day after the doctor's visit, Esther weakly told her husband she felt she was going to die, asked him to kiss her and to give her love to their children. William noticed she was very cold and had barely any heartbeat. Soon after, he formed the opinion she had passed away, washed her face, brushed her hair, carried her upstairs, lay her on a mattress and covered her with a sheet. He then contacted Mr. Myers, the undertaker and his "*insurance chap*", who assured him Esther was covered for £37. Later that morning, he went to tell Dr. Shotton, who was not surprised and issued a death certificate - "*Heart failure brought on by exhaustion*".

The good doctor left his surgery soon afterwards and called at Croft's newsagents. In response to a question, he told them Esther had died, and was then told that she had recently suffered a blow on the head whilst protecting a neighbour's hens from thieves. This was the first he had heard of this, and it caused him to drive his trap to Padiham Police Station and to the Registrar's office to say that it now appeared that an inquest ought to be held.

Meanwhile, James Waddington had come from the undertakers to do what needed to be done. He felt the intense cold of the house and went to measure Esther. Whilst about his business, he saw a movement of her eyelids. Was he mistaken? He thought not and felt her heartbeat - nothing there. However, he noticed a movement of her hand, and had the presence of mind to realise that she wasn't dead - just cold, and drew her to his warm body, rubbing her back vigorously to produce warmth. He shouted to William to "*fetch t'brandy*". Whilst this was being mixed with hot water, he carried Esther downstairs to her bed. In a short time, she "*came round*". Hot water bottles assisted her recovery.

Dr. Shotton re-visited his patient and found her alive - barely. He learnt that, twice previously, as a girl and a woman, she had "died" and received treatment from an undertaker.

A local pub landlord gave Dr. Shotton a sovereign for the death certificate. It was passed to William to buy food, whilst the certificate was passed to the '*Accrington Observer*' editor for publication. When Esther had recovered, she appeared on stage in music halls dressed in black whilst a narrator told her incredible story.

11

ACCRINGTON FIRE BRIGADE & THEIR WORK

John Kelly

Accrington had its own Fire Brigade from 1854 until 1941 when it became part of the National Fire Service. In 1948 the N.F.S. was fragmented and Accrington became a station of the Lancashire County Fire Service. This Borough brigade was separate from those at Clayton, Church and Oswaldtwistle. The full-time and part-time firemen also doubled as ambulance drivers, and attended many fires and *"incidents"*. Some are worthy of mention:-

Friday 1st March 1867.

Miss Letitia Burscough ran a school for children aged 3 to 8 years on the first floor of a building underneath the railway viaduct, close to King Street. On this particular day, 95 of the pupils were present. Entry to the school was by a timber staircase from the ground floor workshop below, which was occupied by Mr. Duckworth who made articles for use in cotton mills. This involved the use of a stove for heating a vat in which *"healds"* were dipped, then hung to dry in the very hot room. It was not uncommon for wax and varnish to boil over onto the stove and ignite. Mr. Duckworth had occupied the premises for only 9 months and had moved there after his previous workshop in Infant Street had burnt down. A nine-year-old boy was responsible for stoking the stove.

At 11am, a child shouted to a teacher that smoke was coming up the stairs. Miss Burscough gave instructions for all to leave. She dragged some children down the stairs and returned four times for more before collapsing. A ladder was put up to an upstairs window and several men ascended it. With their weight, after five children had been rescued, it broke. The Brigade arrived with their horse-drawn engine, drew water from a hydrant near Bull Bridge and controlled the fire. Nine children, including Duckworth's five-year-old daughter, died. Mr. Tatersall later photographed the scene (these must have been amongst the earliest photos taken in Accrington) and one was reproduced in the *'Illustrated London News'*.

In the following months, a new Fire Station was decided upon, to be built at the rear of the new Market Hall. A fire alarm bell was put up on the Peel Institute (which became the Town Hall) and 17 more *"fire plugs"* (hydrants) were installed at locations throughout the town.

Sunday 12th August 1883.

The Borough Brigade had just bought a new steam fire engine for £800. It was needed for an incident which occurred in the late Sunday afternoon in Union Street.

A new 5 ft diameter sewer was being constructed 18 ft below street level. (It wasn't replaced until 1982) 36 year-old Edmund *"Diddler"* Hargreaves was working with another man down in the excavation. He had removed a support prop to help him work more easily, and due to this a large quantity of earth fell on him, pinning him face-down with only his head free. Whilst attempts were made to extricate him, and offers from some colliers from nearby Scaitcliffe Pit were declined, he was given brandy to kill the pain. Meanwhile, it started to rain, and water entered the sewer where Hargreaves lay. Despite the efforts of the new and old engines, the rising water level could not be contained, and he drowned after being trapped for two hours.

Saturday 30th July 1910.

At this period, shops opened until 10 pm each Friday and Saturday, and Williams' Drapery Store in Church Street, at the corner with Holme Street, was open for business for just another 15 minutes. It was a three-storey shop with a basement. 33 females and 2 males worked there, 17 of the girls living on the premises, which were lit by electricity.

One of the large lamps in a window display *"arced"*, and ignited the display. A male employee tried to grab the wire to get it away from the burning cloth. The fire spread rapidly. The horse-drawn brigade turned out from the nearby Market Hall Station just minutes later. The officer in charge was told that all persons were thought to be safely out of the premises, so he concentrated his men's efforts on preventing the fire spreading to adjacent premises. An hour later, a roll-call was conducted, and it was discovered that some ladies were not accounted for. A ladder was put up, entry gained to the premises. Five bodies were found - three shop assistants and two customers, Miss M. Barnes and Mrs. R. Morgan, both Ossie weavers, who had suffocated. The incident highlighted the need for an immediate roll-call to have been made.

Friday 27th April 1917.

The Accrington Brigade went to the assistance of their Church colleagues when an explosion occurred at Blythe's chemical works. This incident became known as the *'Canary Islands Explosion'* and is reported elsewhere in this book.

Thursday 10th January 1924.

Poverty causes men to take risks in order to raise funds for their family's upkeep. James Hoyle made firelighters out of sawdust and napthalene in the kitchen of his house to sell to those who liked something to help their fire get going when they *"beat"* it. On this day, it was snowing. His children, six-year-old Arthur and four-year-old Billy, had no suitable footwear and so didn't go to school. They played with baby Ada (18 months old) in the living room of their cottage in Plantation Mill Square. A large pan of napthalene was on the hob of the fireplace. Mr. Hoyle had Ada under his arm when she accidentally knocked the pan handle on the fireplace, causing the pan to tip. Instantly the room was a mass of fire. James rushed out with Ada, but could not return for the lads because of the heat and smoke. This lasted but a few minutes, during which he tried to get into the house through the front door, but couldn't open it. Later it emerged that the two lads and a dog were wedged behind the door.

An inquest brought in a verdict of *"Accidental Death"*. The Coroner expressed great sympathy but hoped the incident would serve as a warning to others.

❋ ❋ ❋ ❋ ❋ ❋

On 9th May 1935, the Brigade's new Fire Station, with the most up-to-date control system of any in the country was officially opened by a civic party touring the new Courts and Police Station complex in Manchester Road. They witnessed a button being pressed on a fire call being received, whereupon a clock stopped and a graph indicator started, the fire engines (there was space for five) started up, the main doors opened, the alarm rang, the lights came on in the station, the yard and the 12 nearby firemen's houses. They learned that at night it took 110 seconds from receipt of a call to the engines moving off, but this was reduced to 40 seconds in the daytime.

LOCAL FELLOWS & FELONIES

Stephen Greenhalgh & Bob Dobson

Here follows a few of the cases which have occupied the pages of national newspapers in the last century or so:-

1881, Water Street.

James and Malinda Leaver lived in lodgings in Water Street in January 1881 with their two children, six-year-old Henrietta and two-year-old Albert. James was a weaver at nearby Park Shed, and one dinner-time he was seen sharpening a knife. That evening, his wife went with their landlady, Mrs. Smith, to the Tuesday market, leaving the children in bed and James toasting his toes. Mr. Smith returned home at 7-40 pm to find James sitting by the fire. James showed the landlord his knife and told him he had killed Henrietta. Smith quickly established that she was still breathing, though bleeding badly. He ran for a doctor. The police came too and arrested James, who appeared oblivious of all around him. It transpired that he had previously tried to strangle a sleeping man, and had spent some time in asylums.

Sane or insane? The jury decided upon the latter and found him *"Not Guilty"* of murder. He was detained at Her Majesty's pleasure. Had it been murder, it was possibly the first recorded in the district.

1896, Warner Street.

On 9th June 1896, Mrs. Sarah Coates, 61 years, was found murdered at her home, 3 Warner Street. Her husband was a self-employed cabinet maker, employing his son and a 15 year-old apprentice, Christopher Hindle, a tall, well-built lad.

Hindle was sent, on the morning in question, to collect some wood carvings, which he had to take to No.3. He did as he was told. When next seen, about 10-30 am, he rushed into Coates' workshop in Bridge Street and blurted out *"Mrs. Coates is murdered"*. He showed his master and his son a bleeding wound on his right arm.

Father and son rushed home and found Mrs. Coates with her throat cut. Still alive, she was asked who had done this. She replied, *"Nobody"*. At 10-45 am she died. Dr. Clayton surmised that she had been strangled to insensibility, then her throat cut. A peculiar knife was found nearby. It belonged to Mr. Coates, who had last seen it some weeks previously lying on an upstairs window-sill.

Young Christopher was questioned by the Borough Police. He said he had been dusting in the shop (No.3 Warner Street) when he heard screaming upstairs. He rushed up to find a man attempting to strangle Mrs. Coates, saw him cut her throat, then the man lashed out at him viciously with the knife. The man had run off and he had pursued him over the back yard gate, shouting *"Murder"*. He gave a description. When subsequently interviewed, anomalies appeared in his story. He was arrested and charged with murder.

At Lancaster Assizes, Christopher stuck to his story. He was found *"Guilty"* after the judge had *"summed up"* strongly against him. Reading the evidence today, it has to be said that the prosecution did not wholly prove that the lad had done the deed, and that there were doubts arising which he ought to have been given the benefit of.

A petition was started by the *'Accrington Observer'* and signed by thousands. It may have helped sway the Home Secretary to reprieve Christopher Hindle from *"the long drop"*.

1877, 4 Oswald Street, Clayton .

Conditions in the small terraced house were cramped because the occupiers, Michael Kennedy, 50 years, his wife and three children, had lodgers - John and Deborah O'Dowd and their four children. They got on well together, except when Michael was *"in drink"*, when he was aggressive. On Sunday 8th July, Michael had been drinking at a christening, had been refused drink at one pub, but got some more at the *'Hare and Hounds'*, where he was annoyed that John O'Dowd would not drink with him. Michael staggered home, went into No.2 by mistake, and was escorted next door to his own home. Once there, he was dumped in a chair, from which he later rose, lurched over to the fireplace - perhaps he was looking for a heavy poker usually kept there - picked up a heavy chair, swung it round and hit Deborah on the head. She died of concussion of the brain. The chair was broken in the attack.

A jury at the inquest held in the *'Load of Mischief'* pub declared that Kennedy had murdered Deborah. At his trial, just three weeks later, he was found *"Not Guilty"* of murder but *"Guilty"* of manslaughter. He would take no further strong drink for seven years.

1923, Victoria Street.

Since time began, there has been no more awful crime than that which was committed at 12 Victoria Street (to this day still called locally *"t'factory bottom"*) on the afternoon of 18th September 1923.

The house was owned and occupied by Sarah Ann Horbury, a 65 year-old spinster. She had *"lodgers"* - John Whalley, 34 years, his wife Maud and his 5 year-old step-daughter, Agnes Wildman. The couple were not on good terms, probably through Whalley's liking for drink and his dislike of work. He was violent towards his wife, and the previous day she had taken out a summons against him alleging cruelty and neglect. She had often told him that, whatever he might do, she could always earn a living as a weaver through the skill of her hands.

On the morning of this fateful day, Maud had gone to work and taken Agnes to school. She had previously cleared their effects from the marital home. Miss Horbury shouted Whalley from his bed at 11 am, when he left the house, promising to come back later with a handcart for his belongings. He then went to the Poplar Club, where he played billiards and had a pint or two of beer. He was not under the influence of drink when he left about 3 pm. He then went directly to Agnes' school, and told the mistress that he wanted to take Agnes out early to go and stay with relatives in Rishton. Reluctantly, the teacher agreed, and Whalley took the child to No.12.

Arriving home, Agnes shouted for her mother. Her shouting attracted Miss Horbury, who came downstairs to see the pair. When she appeared, Whalley seized a shovel and battered her with it, knocking her unconscious. He then calmly took a *"cut throat"* razor from the drawer and cut Agnes' hands off at the wrists, throwing them under a table. Perhaps he was making sure that, whilst Maud might use her hands to earn a living, her lass would not, and by his action he was attacking his estranged wife. He then attempted suicide.

Sarah Ann came to, crawled out and went to a neighbour's house to raise the alarm. She was seen by 49 year-old Mrs. Parker of 26 Ormerod Street, who collapsed and died from a heart attack on hearing her tale. A passer-by 'phoned the police, who arrived very soon afterwards to find Agnes on the hearth rug, resting her severed limbs on the floor. This probably arrested the bleeding.

Sarah Ann recovered, as did Agnes, who went on to lead a normal life as a schoolgirl and housewife. In spite of her tremendous disadvantage, she taught herself to write, draw and paint beautifully. The crime shocked the nation, and a trust fund was set up to help Agnes. The happenings that day brought shame to the men of Accrington, who declined to say that they came from the town in case others would associate the name with that of John Whalley's vile deed.

Whalley was sentenced to life imprisonment. He had not previously come to the adverse notice of the police.

1934, Marquis Street.

By no means the worst incident in the annals of Accrington's criminal life, but the one which arouses the most interest is what has become known as *"The Bronco Bill murder"*. "Bronco's" real name was William (Bill) Hodson and he acquired his nickname through his practice of wearing a stetson, or cowboy, hat. He had travelled the world as a merchant seaman and fought in the Irish Guards during the Great War. *"He has a wonderful physique - there are very, very few men as strong as he is"*, his solicitor was to say. It didn't come out at his trial, but Bronco did have a reputation as a bully with whom nobody dare argue. He was a member of the *"Blackshirts"*, a Fascist political group. He had a gentle nature too, particularly at home with his family. 41 years old, he lived in Beech Grove, up Spring Hill. His parents had the chip shop in Whalley Road at the bottom of Maudsley Street.

Bronco's victim in the incident to be related was Joe Hurley, a 38 year-old steeplejack who, on the 21st December, was working as a telephone cable layer, as was Hodson. They probably saw each other on the afternoon of that last Friday before Christmas. Having been paid, Hodson and some others were *"laid off"*. Undoubtedly, Hodson knew Hurley, who was the admitted father of a child born some years previously to Charlotte, who later married Hodson. That child had been adopted. The Hodsons were a contented couple with a 6 years-old child.

On the Friday evening, both men had been drinking, separately, in the local pubs. Hurley was in *'The Commercial'* and *'The Hope & Anchor'* before going to *'The Castle'* where he would hear Hodson talking loudly of his dislike for Catholics and the Irish. Hurley was of Irish Catholic stock. Neither man was drunk, though Bronco was the more affected. From *'The Castle'*, both went with their mates to the *'Slaters'Arms'*, a rough pub sited at the top of Marquis Street, almost next door to *'The Hope & Anchor'*, and which was knocked down to allow for the creation of Broadway a year or so later. Joe Hurley was also a strong man, though of moderate temperament. He had been awarded a Military Medal for bravery when fighting with the East Lancashire Regiment during the Great War. Having left the pub - it was now eleven o'clock - the pair exchanged words, and in a back street behind *'The Slaters'Arms'*, they shaped up for a fight. Bronco took off his overcoat jacket, and with one of his punches knocked Joe to the ground. He then jumped on him, took hold of his head and banged it several times on the stone setts. Getting up, he *"used his head for a football"*, then *"jumped on his head like a madman"*. William Myers witnessed much of this from his bedroom window at 8 Marquis Street and heard Bronco shouting *"I'll kill him"*. Bronco left Joe with the small crowd which had gathered. Someone carried him to his home at 6 Cobden Street, just a spit and a stride away.

PC Sargeson was called out by a caller at the Police Station near the Town Hall. He went to the scene on his motor cycle combination and there he saw Bronco, noticing that he wasn't drunk when he told him of the fight there had been. No arrest was made. Bronco called at the Police Station a couple of hours later, but wasn't arrested. In fact, he wasn't detained until 5-30 am on the Sunday morning, 23rd December (30 hours after the fight), when Inspector Nathan Todd and Detective Sergeant Whewell called at his home to tell him that Hurley had died. Hodson was charged with manslaughter, and that charge was not changed to murder until 11th January on Home Office advice.

Hodson's trial at Manchester Assizes two months later lasted just a few days, at the end of which the foreman of the jury announced *"Guilty of wilful murder with a strong recommendation for mercy"*. Bill told the black-capped judge *"I am innocent, my Lord"*.

Bearing in mind the jury's comment and the circumstances of the case, the Home Secretary substituted *"life imprisonment"* for the death penalty, and Bronco settled down to prison life. However, after just over seven years, on 13th July 1942, he was released on licence, a form of parole. It is said that this was because he had saved the life of a warder in a prison riot or fire. Whatever the circumstances, if they existed or not, the reason for his early release is not shown in the file relating to him kept in the Public Record Office. It may be that the war, then halfway through, had something to do with the Home Office decision, but Bill must have been regarded as a reformed man. He didn't come to police notice again, preferring the comforts of his wife and family to all else. My own view is that he doesn't deserve to be known as a murderer.

1974, Manchester Road, Baxenden.

At 4 am on the 6th September, Derek Astin, the Baxenden postmaster, was disturbed in his bedroom by a hooded man armed with two guns. Derek got out of bed to tackle the intruder, who was searching for the Post Office keys. In the struggle, Derek was fatally wounded. The crime was similar to several raids at post offices throughout the country, and a massive police effort was put into detecting the crime. Soon, a name was linked with the crimes committed by a stealthy man in a black hood - *"the Black Panther"*, and soon his real name was known - Donald Neilson. After his visit to Accrington in a stolen van, Neilson went on to commit more serious crime, including the kidnapping of a 17 year-old heiress, Lesley Whittle. Eventually, Neilson was locked up by two diligent village bobbies.

AN EVIL NUISANCE

In the issue of Saturday 7th April 1860, the Accrington Free Press told of some inhabitants of Warner Street having recently sent a petition to the Local Board of Health. It read *"We, the inhabitants of Warner Street beg to draw the attention of your honourable board to a great nuisance which exists on the East side of Warner Street. For a number of years, hawkers, auctioneers and pot dealers have made a practice of occupying one half of the above mentioned street. The filth and straw finds any egress into the shops on both sides of the street, while the noise and the obstruction is becoming so great that we pray your honourable board to take the matter into your serious consideration and endeavour to remove the evil nuisance at the end of Manchester Road"*.

The original grievances arose through a pot stall being stationed in Warner Street, where the owner of it sold a great variety and quantity of pots. It is interesting that the writers refer to *Abbey Street* as *Manchester Road*. Nine years later, the market was moved to a permanent hall and ground.

THE MARKET HALL

What today we call the *'Market Hall'* was called *'The Market House'* when it was opened on 23rd October 1869. The design was the best of 15 submitted by architects from around the country, and was that of James Francis Boyle of Liverpool.

On 16th May 868, the Local Board of health, under their chairman Samuel Dugdale, held a stone-laying ceremony, preceded by a procession. Headed by a police contingent, it contained two bands, the Church Artillery Volunteers, tradesmen, Free Masons and Operative Masons, the Fire Brigade and their engines, Oddfellows, Foresters, Free Mechanics, Rechabites, Ancient Shepherds - and Mr. Briggs with his printing apparatus. This information comes from a leaflet *"Printed (by Authority) in the procession, by Mr. J. J. Briggs"*.

The fine building, a wonderful example of the mason's craft, is 183 feet long, 120 feet wide, 38 feet high, rising to 48 feet at the front. It cost £28,300. The masonry and joinery contracts went to Accrington firms, as did that for plumbing and glazing - Doctor Carter got that one. This was not a medical man *"doing a foreigner"*, but a man whose Christian name was Doctor. He was possibly the seventh child, or it may be that his parents had indulged in the popular fashion of giving their lad a Christian name associated with a profession.

Despite the drizzle, over 6,000 Sunday School scholars and others took part in the procession and the opening ceremony, making it the most impressive event seen in the town up to that time.

MEMORIES OF ACCRINGTON MARKET

Benita Moore

Accrington has been a market town for centuries, the earliest evidence appearing in the Court Rolls of Clitheroe for 1547, where mention is made of the *'King's Market'* of Accrington. Our splendid Market Hall dates from 1869. It was originally planned to build a market in the Barnes Street area of the town, but this was decided against, as it was not central. Warner Street used to be the old shopping area of the town until the market was moved to the site in front of the Market Hall with stalls round Peel Street. Thus, for countless years the canvas-covered stalls delighted the residents of Accrington and surrounding towns. The new *'Umbrella Market'* opened in 1962 on Broadway.

Having been born in Church just before the 2nd World War, Accrington was the Metropolis - the 'London' - of East Lancashire in my small world. I can remember how the weekly visit to Accrington Market excited me. The delightful sights and sounds, tastes and smells still stand out clearly in my memory. Although there was a war on and things were scarce and on ration, I never failed to find some new delight to satisfy my childish curiosity or appetite.

All week, after listening to grim news and conforming to austere rules, the weekly visit to Accrington Market and its ensuing pleasures shone like a beacon in an otherwise bleak wartime childhood, necessitated by rationing and lack of goods. Nobody near us had a car, everyone either walked to town or used the bus, boarded at the *'Church Commercial'* stop. This was a special treat for the children of my age. Mother worked, so we had slightly more money to spend than some other families. Even so, she was always adamant that we got good value for money and whatever we could scrounge out of the meagre war rations. She was a very good manager and would scour the market stalls for good meat or any material that could be made into clothes.

After the washing and cleaning were completed on a Saturday morning, mother would say: *"Right, get ready"*, and off we'd go to catch the bus to Accrington Market, with me peering eagerly through the bus windows as we passed the rows of terraced streets, Sacred Heart Church, the Grammar School, the old railway arch and the Town Hall until finally we arrived at the market.

In winter, the canvas-covered stalls, with snow on their tops, looked like little Swiss Chalets or Christmas Houses to my childish eyes, whilst the *'wooden green stalls on wheels'*, as we knew them, were especially fascinating.

I remember the market more in winter than in summer, as the warmth and excitement it generated seemed to last through the whole winter months. First we'd visit the outside stalls. I remember some of the names that have been part of Accrington Market for generations and some which until comparatively recently have remained. Southworth's tripe stall was one such, and in winter, mother always made a beeline for this and bought tripe from John and Annie Cook (Southworth's daughter and son-in-law). This was taken home and cooked in milk in the frying pan with onions which, together with home fried chips, provided a tasty and nourishing meal. There was another tripe stall - Eccles' which was worked by Florrie and Ivy - two sisters whom I know to this day. In previous years, mother told me there had been a *'Balloon Man'* selling his wares to children, but there was a war on, so he had disappeared. However, there were still small portions of delicious hot

19

peas and black puddings to be had.

The queues at some of the stalls during the war were horrendous, and the long wait was often not very justifiable. Furey's stall was one of the favourites for fruit and vegetables, and I can once remember waiting in a queue at their stall for almost an hour, because we had heard they had some bananas. I'd never *seen* a real banana, never mind *tasted* one! I kept looking across at the lighted windows of Woolworth's store whilst we waited but alas, the wait was in vain. When we did eventually reach the head of the queue we were told: *"Sorry, no bananas left"*. Then: *"How many in your family?"* *"Two adults, two children"*, replied my mother. We were handed two apples and two oranges, our share of the meagre ration. Not the stall holders fault, but I was so disappointed, I burst into tears, as I actually wanted to see a banana! The rest of the outside market was like a fairyland to me. There were button stalls with a few coloured ribbons and scraps of wool, shiny buttons and reels of bright cotton, needles and pins, darning stools, and material bits which mother could turn into skirts, underslips or even knickers. Round in Peel Street, there was a hardware stall which smelt of firelighters and sold candles, tapers, nightlights, spills (to light the gas with), bundles of firewood, dolly blues, donkey stones and a myriad of other cheap and useful household items, as well as the conventional pots and pans, keys, string and chains. I can well remember looking for any unusual buttons on one stall and using some of my weekly 2d to buy them. Over the years, I built up quite a collection of these in a small tin box which was part of my hoard of treasured possessions.

Further up Peel Street, opposite where the two entries to the new market are now and at the corner of Infant and Peel Streets, was another part of the market, but indoors this time. This housed such notable names as Catlow's (fruit and veg.) and, most important of all to me, Stockley's sweet stall. This was the place for me to spend part of my weekly sweet ration. I would browse around the stall, watching the lady with the little hammer breaking caramel toffee into small pieces. Should I buy some of this or something that lasted longer such as aniseed balls or sarsaparilla tablets? The choice wasn't great because of the war, but I meant to get value for money and something which would last me all week. In the end, mother would get so fed up of waiting that she'd make the choice for me.

I can remember the day sweets came off ration and we went down to Accrington Market. I went round every toffee stall I could see, Lythe's, and the one which sold Tom Hodgson's and Lightbown's sweets and, of course, Stockley's. I'd been saving money for weeks for this great day and must have bought 3lbs of sweets at each stall.

Getting back to when I was four or five years old though, my weekly trips to Accrington Market with mother became more and more interesting as I explored the stalls with an enquiring mind. On wet days, the stalls would drip dismally, sending shoots of cold water down the back of your neck if you didn't wear a hat. In winters which were then invariably cold and freezing, I would hardly recognise the familiar faces as they were huddled in hand-knitted balaclavas, woollen hats and mufflers, scarves and voluminous coats. After we'd been outside and collected our fruit and veg. ration, we'd go into the Market Hall where further delights enthralled me. The treat of the week, in winter, was a hot drink at Stock's cordial stall. A hot peppermint or a Vimto or blackcurrant revived a numb limb and brightened the long wait in the endless queues. The Co-op also had a stall in one corner of the Market Hall, selling bread and cakes as well as other popular items.

Accrington Market Hall was, and still is, a magnificent building. Its inside stalls and facilities were a paradise for a wartime child. Some of the original meat and other stalls still exist today; although some are owned by different people. Some well-known names are: Feathers (butchers), Chadwicks (butchers), Greenwood's (cheeses), Grime Brothers (butchers), the old wool stall, Jones' cut glass. There was Billy Pearson's, Fairbrother's biscuit stall, the hat stall run for many years by Marion Makepeace, the toffee stall where Joe and Nora Hargreaves traded for many years, Trickett's Ices, Adam's, Matthew's (hardware) stall and many, many more. Peggy's Cafe in the corner was a favourite with me, as sometimes mother would take me in and buy me a delicious helping of hot pot or sometimes sponge pudding as a special treat. There was also the Palatine Cafe, Whitewell Dairies and Lomax's Cafe which were very popular. The lights from the stalls glittered and sparkled like fairy-lights, compared with the 'black-outs' we had to endure at home. Mother would always be on the look-out for a bargain and I still have a small crystal vase, much prized by her, which was a 'bargain' from Jones' china stall. The hat stall was also a favourite of mine, as I'd be fascinated by women of all ages trying on feathered, woollen, felt and straw hats. I'd watch their expressions as they paraded themselves in front of the big mirror inside the stall, trying to improve their looks with whatever hat was available at the price they could afford.

After the war, things improved tremendously. Stalls both in the Market Hall and outside on the open market were given a face-lift and vastly improved. Yet the atmosphere was still there! The hustle, the bustle, the smells and the colourful sights and sounds were still magic to me. The choice of goods improved, and we had Len's cooked meats (now run by his grandson, Greg), Whitewell Dairies, which had been there originally, but was much updated, Doug's (ladies underwear), Lestor's stocking stall, Andy's florists and George Cropper's butchers stall. The flower stall run by Margaret Hayes (nee Furey) was a colourful

Accrington.

The Market.

The Wrench Series, No. 6956.

The fine Market Hall appeared on many postcards in the days before the First World War.

21

spectacle and Margaret only retired a few years ago. The market used to open until 8 or 9 o'clock at night in earlier years, but these hours were reduced gradually to bring it in line with other shops.

In my early teens I was living in Oswaldtwistle. My friend and I would catch the bus on a Saturday morning and pay 6d to visit the Odeon Club at the cinema on Broadway, which was a jolly good show of about 2 hours duration. Afterwards we had more spending money left to go round the market and take our choice of Oxo or Horlicks, ice cream or maybe a vanilla, a bar of Fry's chocolate cream or maybe some Holland's toffee. We would spend the whole afternoon mooching around the stalls, savouring the atmosphere, free at last to examine and purchase as we liked, with no rationing restrictions.

In 1955, when I was 17, I started work as an assistant at Accrington Library and on market days (Tuesdays, Fridays and Saturdays), weather permitting, I'd take my sandwiches and walk round the market during my lunch hour. Times were changing, and so were the market stalls. More sophisticated stalls appeared, including that great character, **Uncle Dick**, from Blackpool who sold some of the best bargains ever. I could spend my dinner hour just standing munching my sandwiches, watching and listening to him. His technique of selling anything from a clock to a suitcase was superb. A bewildering array of goods appeared during this era, as restrictions were lifted and Britain rejoiced in the aftermath of the grim war years. Accrington Market traders, always wonderful salesmen, were not slow to take to this new consumer boom.

But the wind of change was in the offing. In the late 1950s, the town council decided that the *'old fashioned'* Market should be moved from its Peel Street and front-of-Market Hall site to a more fashionable one built on the Broadway site. With the culverting of the Hyndburn, this became possible and in 1962 the new *'umbrella style'* market was opened - a concrete structure covering the stalls. Old habits and customs die hard in a traditional town like Accrington though, and it took the townspeople quite some time to adjust to this new structure, but it was nice to see some of the familiar old stalls in their new places. The Market Hall at that time remained untouched, but in 1987 was given a face-lift and refurbishment which enhanced its beauty both inside and out. It is a building of outstanding beauty and architecture and local citizens are justly proud of it. I still enjoy sitting outside the impressive structure, savouring the beauty of the chestnut trees, which by May are in their full glory, on a sunny day, whilst inside, the traditional stalls still carry on their excellent service. Many of the stalls have, of course, changed hands, and also their products, but the old atmosphere still pervades over the Lancashire people who continue to shop at the same stalls that their mothers and grandmothers did, years ago.

With the coming of the Supermarkets, the old -fashioned *'traditional'* markets in Lancashire have had to *'look to their laurels'*, but Accrington has always had a faithful band of followers, devoted to their own particular stalls and tradesmen, and I am one of them, I'm happy to say. What of the future? Plans are already being discussed by Hyndburn Council to relocate the market to where it was originally - on Peel Street and in front of the Market Hall. The wheel has turned full circle, and maybe it will be back to the 'olden days' for Accrington Market once again. Whatever happens, of one thing I'm quite sure, the memories of Accrington Market and the pleasures it gave me as a child, and as an adult, will stay firmly etched in my memory for the rest of my life.

OWD JOHN BRIDGE, SEXTON & FAMILY MAN

Jack Broderick

When glancing through the old accounts books of St. James' Church, a name which frequently occurs is that of John Bridge, the sexton. He seems to have been a very reliable general factotum who looked after the day-to-day running of the church premises. Each year about the time of the annual vestry meeting he prepared a list of items purchased and small bills paid during the previous year.

Several items occur yearly, such as *'new almanac, 2d'* at New Year. A bottle of ink for the vestry cost 6d, oil for the bells 6d and oil for the clock one shilling. Candles for the church and ringers were 6d a pound. *'Chips'* i.e. kindling wood for the stoves, came to five shillings for a year. Details of church cleaning include *'soft soap and potash for pews, 9d'*, *'new brush and steale 4s 6d'* and the daily rate for a cleaner was half a crown. Many items were for minor repairs in and about the church, e.g. repairing pews, replacing roof slates and window glass (frequently) and repairing as well as washing the minister's *'surplus'* (surplice).

The vestry stove seems to have required regular attention by William Tasker, the blacksmith, in order to make it capable of consuming the large quantities of coal that came from Woodnook and Altham, and sometimes Dunkenhalgh Pits. Consequently, the chimney had to be swept regularly, and this is shown as *'sut clening hought of draft, 1s 9d'*. *'Sweeping the church (for one year), 3s 0d'*, *'Clening & streighteng for Bishop, 10s'* tells us that spit and polish were not unknown in ecclesiastical circles. John may also have been a bell-ringer, as in 1850 is the item *'tolling for Sir Robert Peel, 5s'*. This mark of respect was for the Prime Minister, who died on 29th June. He was the nephew of Jonathan Peel, who built Accrington House.

Other duties assigned to John were the care of the graveyard and digging graves. John purchased locks for the gates, a reminder of the necessity for security at that time when disinterments were possible. The grave ladder, wheelbarrows, spades and hacks were all repaired rather than replaced. Such frugality was typical of those times.

After reading through John's accounts and becoming accustomed to his handwriting and phonetic spelling, I found myself wanting to know more about him as a person. Accordingly, I consulted the parish registers and found the entry, *'John, son of Adam and Jennet Bridge, born December 27th 1797, baptised January 1st 1798'*. Jennet, his mother, was a member of the Lang family. Her brother, Jacob, was mine host at the **'Red Lion'** in Abbey Street. In 1841, John was living with his wife Charlotte and their daughter Sarah, aged 5 years, in Warner Street. He was a shoemaker who had been apprenticed to William Booth. In the same year, his father, Adam, then 75 years-old, was living with John's brother, Jacob, in Plantation Square. Both were printshop workers at Plantation Mill. Amongst brother Jacob's family of small children were two boys who were to become two of Accrington's *'Captains of Industry'* - Lang Bridge and Joseph William Bridge.

There is a sadder tale to tell of John the sexton. It is inscribed on the stone over his grave in the churchyard he tended for 28 years. Charlotte, his wife, died before him ,aged 47 years, in 1845. Also listed are his nine children, Reuben, Abel, Jane, Aaron, John, Joseph and Mary (twins) and Abraham and Sarah (twins). They were all buried before they had reached their sixth birthday. John Bridge died 4th March 1866 aged 66 years, and was one of the last to be buried in St. James' Churchyard before it was closed for earth burials on December 28th 1866.

JOHN WILSON, INVENTOR & ENTREPRENEUR

Practical businessman and inventor, John Wilson came to Accrington from Kendal as a young chap and started an ironmongery business in Church Street. About the same time, he went into partnership with Alderman J. Barlow and in 1925 they bought the Ritz Cinema, which Wilson owned until his death in 1954, aged 69 years. In the 1930s, he opened the Ritz Ballroom, later selling it to Howard & Bullough's for use as a club. He served on Church Council for 25 years and was chairman from 1941 to 1946. Wilson Square, Church, is named in his memory.

His fame as an inventor (he held a dozen patents) was assured when he gave a demonstration in court of his *'Iceland Freezer'*, patented in 1923 for the making of icecream, when someone had doubted his claim as to its speed and efficiency. In 1928, he introduced to the world a new gramophone and gramo-radio, made in Church by *'The Gramo-Radio Company'*. He opened showrooms in Cannon Street *'where those interested in sound reproduction will be able to hear for themselves this invention, for which a promising future is prophesied'*. Other inventions included a soda-water producer, a silent railway line and a water-pump system. All this went on whilst he was running the Ritz and the Queen's Cinemas, introducing to local cinema-goers the joys of *'talkies and 3-D'*. He was a member of local Water, Sewerage and Cemetery committees, and a philanthropist to the people of Church.

In 1903, at a Blackburn theatre, *'Houdini'* appeared and challenged the audience to chain him beyond escape. John Wilson took up the gauntlet and succeeded in beating the challenge - then he escaped from Houdini's own handcuffs.

THE TIN WHISTLE MAN

Roy Pearson

Before the advent of the *'Beeching Era'*, when the finest railway network in the world was butchered, leading to today's road chaos, Accrington was an important junction. Trains ran direct to Manchester up the infamous Baxenden Bank - one of the steepest railway climbs in Britain - and there was a flourishing goods traffic in the Scaitcliffe, Eagle and Paxton Street areas. At the bottom of Ormerod Street, where it meets Scaitcliffe Street, was a railway bridge similar to that at the other end near Paxton Street but much more dangerous. In fact it was so dangerous that even the little traffic of those days required the use of one of the few sets of traffic lights in the town.

It was a dark, damp, smelly, noisy and dismal place. It was dark because it was overshadowed on one side by the huge bulk of Bullough's and on the other by the pit - Scaitcliffe Colliery. It was damp because the water trickled down the walls from the railway above and dripped from the steel girders of the bridge to leave deposits like small icicles behind. It was smelly because there was a dreadfully insanitary gentlemen's urinal on the corner of Eagle Street. It was noisy because of the echoing walls, the occasional train overhead and, at times, the almost incessant shunting of a little saddle tank based at the loco-shed in Charter Street, the most important such shed in the district. And it was dismal because of all these factors.

But it was a major thoroughfare, for in those days the lines to Manchester and Blackburn effectively cut-off a section of the town, being pierced by only five bridges of which this was one. Perhaps because of this and the resulting prospect of trade and being outside the town centre where the police were more in evidence, it was the site chosen by the Tin Whistle Man.

Who, or what he was, I never knew. Maybe he was an injured soldier from the War, though I never noticed any infirmity; maybe someone just out to earn extra money, for goodness knows there was little enough of it about in most families in those days; maybe just someone down on his luck and living rough. Whatever the reason, he must have been desperate to have stood there in the cold and damp of a winter's Saturday night playing his little tin whistle for ha'pennies or, if lucky, a penny or two. Did he play on other nights? I never knew, for Saturday was the only night we went that way on our regular visit to the Ritz cinema. But every winter's Saturday night I would hear the shrill notes of his little tin whistle as we passed the bottom of Fountain Street, unless they were drowned by the noise of the railway. As we got closer it would get louder and assume the recognisable form of a tune, usually a jig, so suited to the instrument. I came to associate him with Saturday nights, in winter that is, for I can never recall seeing him except in the glow of streetlamps. He became as much a part of the scene as the cold, dark walk to the pictures, the sweets we saved for Saturday night to eat whilst watching the *'Three Stooges'* - a Ritz speciality - and a shouted conversation with my uncle who worked the winding gear at the pit.

To a child's eyes, the Tin Whistle Man always seemed enormous in his long, threadbare coat, yet his presence was strangely re-assuring. I always felt sorry for him having to stand there in such a forlorn and unappealing place, but I was grateful for the touch of brightness that his simple tunes brought to one of the most drab corners of the town.

One Saturday night he wasn't there. Nothing to worry about, he often disappeared with the coming of Spring and he'd be back the next Winter. But he wasn't, nor the next, and I never saw him again.

Scaitcliffe Street bridge, in the shadow of 'Bullough's', carried the railway line from Accrington to Baxenden. *(Accrington Library Local History Collection)*

25

THE MISSING HISTORY OF ACCRINGTON

Alan Pickering

Several years ago, I found, amongst the pages of a history book, a prospectus advertising a book called *'A History of Accrington Old & New, and the Neighbourhood, including Church, Oswaldtwistle, Haslingden, Baxenden, Huncoat, Hapton, Altham, Clayton-le-Moors, Oakenshaw and Rishton'*. The prospectus went on to say that 'the book is now preparing for the press'. I was perplexed by this, as in years of collecting local history material, I had not seen, or even heard of, this book. Intrigued, I decided to try to find out what became of the book and its author. The prospectus, an impressive item in itself, is a four-page advertisement issued in the 1880s. It includes a list of subscribers, including such toffs as the Duke of Devonshire, the Duke of Buccleuch and Queensbury, the Marquis of Hartington, the Earl of Derby and William Abram, who wrote the monumental *'History of Blackburn'* in 1877. It was inside this book that the prospectus was found.

The author of the book was Rev. John Robert Boyle of Cottingham, near Hull, who, the prospectus states, *'has been engaged in gathering material for several years'*. One of Accrington's later historians, Richard Ainsworth, in his book *'Old Homesteads of Accrington'* (1928), gives no mention of Boyle or his work; in fact he states there is scant material recorded of Accrington's past, a statement he surely would not have made had Boyle's book been published. We must accept that the book, - *'no element in the history of the district will be neglected'* - must have foundered.

If it foundered, - why? And what became of the manuscript and author?

John Robert Boyle was the grandson of John Riley, owner of a bookshop in Accrington about 1818, who was also a printer with a print-works at Broad Oak. Young John Robert worked at his grandfather's business at Broad Oak for a short time until he was old enough to be packed off to Manchester Grammar School. After leaving there, he became a Swedenborgian minister. By this time he was also a well-known and much respected.

He became City Archivist at Hull, where he preached, and wrote several books on the history of Hull and Humberside. His job as City Archivist was to prove his downfall, for during his duties translating and recording ancient manuscripts he came across some interesting letters and documents written by the 17th-century poet, Andrew Marvell. These became too much of a temptation for him, and he stole them, later submitting them to a London auction house. There, they were recognised by an observant person who associated them with Hull Corporation. A check found them to be missing from the archives. Rev. Boyle, now *'found out'*, was arrested, sent for trial, found *'Guilty'* and sent to prison. The effect on him was devastating, for on his release he was in poor health. With this, and no income, he was sent to the workhouse infirmary, where he died six weeks later, aged 54 years, sad, disgraced and broken.

Rev. Boyle was a minister, historian, archaeologist and author. He was also a bachelor whose love in life was books. It was this *'History of Accrington Parish'*, which took years of preparation, that most likely brought about his downfall, for I suspect that the income raised from the stolen letters was to finance publication of his book about his home town. Who knows, stored away in some forgotten archive, there may still survive the lost manuscript of the now-forgotten *'History of Accrington'*. I hope it does exist and one day comes to light, for it cost so much to John Robert Boyle, an Accrington lad.

DR. JONATHAN BAYLEY
THE SWEDENBORGIAN CHURCH IN ACCRINGTON
Martin J. Crossley Evans

In the nineteenth century, Accrington had the most numerous congregation of Swedenborgians in England. The importance of the town to the movement and the dramatic increase in membership of the Swedenborgian, New Jerusalem or more simply the New Church was largely due to one man, the Rev. Jonathan Bayley (1810-1886), pastor of the church in Accrington between 1834 and 1855. His biographer, the Rev. John Presland, stated that Dr. Bayley's influence was such that most of the important men in the town attended the New Church during his ministry and in the succeeding decades of the century.

Emanuel, Baron von Swedenborg (1688-1772), was a Swedish mining specialist, mathematician, astronomer, philosopher, metaphysician, religious mystic and advanced thinker. The father of crystallography, he also designed prototypes of the submarine, airship and the magazine-attached gun. Swedenborg believed that he was in constant contact with angels and the souls of the dead.

Although Swedenborg did not found a church, his followers organized one in London in 1787. They believed that Swedenborg had been called by God to disclose the spiritual meaning of the Scriptures to the world. Swedenborg's teachings were offensive to many Christians, and his published works, such as *'Concerning Conjugal Love'*, were under frequent attack. Dr. Bayley, as the representative of the New Jerusalem Church in Accrington, was often drawn into polemic battles in pulpit and press, where he was called upon to defend particular doctrines. He did this convincingly and with considerable vigour.

Swedenborg's doctrines and teaching attracted numerous supporters in the first half of the nineteenth century, particularly in Lancashire and Yorkshire. By 1853 there were about 80 societies in England. The church's doctrines were promulgated by the New Jerusalem Missionary and Tract Society, the New Church Free School Society, the Swedenborgian Association and the Society for the Publication of New Church Doctrines, and by about seventy-five ministers.

The Swedenborgian Society in Accrington was founded in the early years of the nineteenth century. The first chapel was opened in 1807, but the society made little progress at first. By 1834 it numbered 43 members in a town of between six and seven thousand people. In the April of that year Jonathan Bayley rode from Manchester on horseback and supplied the place of the expected preacher, who was unable to attend. Within a few months he had been called to the pastorate, moved to Accrington, and opened both a private and night school in the town, which enabled him to support his wife and family. Bayley's humour, buoyancy, and positive approach to problems soon won him influential friends and supporters in the town. Although he inherited a small congregation, he was able to raise the funds for a larger and more versatile Sunday School, which was opened on the day of his ordination in 1836. Bayley was a gifted and charismatic teacher, and the school had an active and highly successful life in the building for almost half a century. When it was replaced by a larger structure in 1885, Jonathan Bayley, then a successful London preacher, was invited by the society in Accrington to visit the town and lay its foundation stone.

He went on to found the New Jerusalem Sunday School Union in 1840, and to serve as editor of *'The Juvenile Magazine'* between 1842 and 1852, thus extending his influence well beyond Accrington. The evening school run by him was claimed by his biographer as 'the direct precursor of the Accrington Mechanics' Institute'.

Soon after his arrival in Accrington, Dr. Bayley was obliged to assume the mantle of an apologist when his church and its doctrines were attacked by two Baptist preachers, Messrs. Worrall and Poynder, who challenged the doctrine of the Resurrection which was preached in his chapel (1836). In 1844 a Methodist local preacher, Mr. Figg, *'virulently assailed the doctrine of the Atonement'* as interpreted by Swedenborg and his followers. In both controversies Dr. Bayley had the better of his opponents. His congregation consequently increased.

The doctrines of the Swedenborgians were not only disseminated through the publicity they received through Dr. Bayley's controversies with Messrs. Worrall, Poynder and Figg, and the services he conducted in Accrington on Sundays and on Wednesday evenings. On Tuesday evenings he either rode or walked the six miles to Burnley to preach to the small society there, and once a fortnight he undertook the eighteen mile round trip to Clitheroe. Until these towns were accessible by railway, evening journeys required determination and stamina.

Dr. Bayley's involvement in the life of Accrington included his advocacy of the principles of the Temperance Movement, and his active support for the British and Foreign Bible Society. In common with most Nonconformists, he adhered in politics to the Liberals. He was an active member of the Anti-Corn Law League in the late 1830s and 1840s, speaking on the same platform as Richard Cobden and John Bright, the leading advocates for the repeal of the Corn Laws, which regulated the importation of foreign wheat and kept prices of home grown wheat artificially high in order to benefit the landlords and farmers. Dr. Bayley championed the cause of the poor, who were the main beneficiaries of the repeal of the Corn Laws in 1846.

One of Dr. Bayley's chief pleasures, in addition to nature and gardens, was travel. He was widely travelled in Europe and spent most of his summer holidays on the Continent. He was well acquainted with Germany and, as dissenters were unable to study at Oxford or Cambridge, he decided to take his degree there. In 1850 he received the degree of Doctor of Philosophy from the University of Tubingen for a thesis on the Hebrew of the Book of Job. Upon resigning his place in Accrington in 1855, Dr. Bayley travelled to Dresden and studied the national system of education in Saxony and other German states.

Dr. Bayley's ministry turned the Accrington society into the largest gathering of Swedenborgians in Great Britain. The old chapel was inadequate to provide seating for all who attended, so on 24th June 1849, a larger chapel was opened. In July 1867 a gallery was added to the building. Dr. Bayley, who by this time was ministering in London, was the preacher at the re-opening of the chapel.

Although Dr. Bayley was resident in London from 1856 onwards, he retained a keen interest in Lancashire affairs. He often travelled to Accrington at election time to vote and to speak on behalf of the Liberal candidate. He preached the first charity sermon in London at the start of the Cotton Famine to raise money to relieve the cotton working operatives.

Dr. Bayley's pastorate at Argyle Chapel lasted for sixteen years. In 1872 he began his third pastorate at the Palace Gardens Church, Kensington, where he doubled the congregation to 302 members, making it the largest New Church society in England after Accrington. Whilst there he founded the New Church Orphanage and revised the Church's Liturgy and Hymn Book. He became ill on holiday in France, and died shortly afterwards in 1886, at the age of seventy-six. His funeral at Highgate Cemetery was attended by a deputation from Accrington who paid generous and well-earned tributes to Dr. Bayley's life and ministry among them.

THE OSSIE BOMBER

In January 1923, a report in the *'Accrington Observer'* told of *'an unemployed man with a grievance, real or fancied, rushed into the Council Chamber of Oswaldtwistle Town Hall on Thursday afternoon, and, brandishing in his hand a Mills grenade, as used in the war, exclaimed "I'll blow the......lot of you to blazes".'*

The councillors had been discussing ways and means of providing employment when he burst in. Councillor Abel Bury, a building contractor, recognised the man as George Hindle (though the paper did not name him), a master bricklayer and stone mason who he had previously employed. Mr. Bury took hold of Hindle, ignoring the fact that he had pulled the pin on the grenade and was threatening to use a gun he said he had in his pocket. He bundled George, a powerfully-built man in his 30s, out into the corridor and bolted the door.

The anticipated explosion didn't occur, and, looking through the chamber windows, the frightened town elders saw George in the road still brandishing the bomb and threatening to hurl it at the building. *'Then he took to his heels and ran off'*. The reporter called him *'a frenzied intruder'*.

The police were called and investigated. They found the grenade was a harmless relic of the war *'in which he had played his part'*, and had been kept on the mantel-piece at home as a souvenir. The councillors later discussed the incident *'and saw the humour of the situation'*.

There wasn't any humour in it for George. He was a proud, honest, fully-skilled tradesman with no work to feed his wife and two daughters. Besides fighting and being wounded in the war, he had been to America in search of work, and had left his brother there. A good-living Ossie lad, he was boisterous, liked a pint and had been known to heckle Mr. Lewis, the Blackburn Temperance worker. His family thought he had brought shame on them, and declined to discuss the incident in later years. When times improved, George worked on many local buildings, including the wall around Rishton Cricket Club - there's no finer example of the bricklayer's craft - and ended up in the employ of *'Bullough's'* where his skills were recognised.

Aye, he were a rum bugger, mi grandad.

BIRTH OF A LEGEND

John C Goddard

From time to time statements are made claiming that one of the most famous outlaws of the American wild west was born in Accrington. Is this true, or is it a story partly based on true facts but which has been added to, modified or misheard as it has passed from person to person? Or perhaps it is simply a case of misplaced pride or a need for reflected glory.

Most of us will have seen young American missionaries about Accrington or even had them knocking at our doors. These young people, Elders of the Church of Latter Day Saints, have been successful in forming churches in neighbouring towns. But it comes as quite a surprise to discover that these visits are not just a recent occurrence. The Mormon church was founded by Joseph Smith in 1830 and by 1836 the first missionaries were already preaching in Lancashire and are recorded as holding services in Huncoat in the 1840s.

One of their early converts was a young weaver in Burnley by the name of Robert Parker. He had his eye on a girl who worked in the same mill and they started courting. Anne Hartley came from Nelson and was a year older than Robert. Her parents weren't very happy about Robert's religious beliefs and possibly Anne herself wasn't ever deeply committed but she became a convert and joined the Latter Day Saints. Shortly afterwards, in May 1843, she married Robert Parker and they came to live in Accrington where they found work in one of the weaving sheds. They made a home in a cottage at Waterflats which was situated in the area now covered by the hospital. Here they began to raise a family, their first son, Maximilian, being born in early June 1844. The census return for 1851 shows Robert aged 31, a warper; Anne his wife aged 32; Maximilian aged 6; Martha Alice aged 4 and Arthur aged 11 months. Two other children, Margaret and Emily, were born in Accrington but died in their first year.

Robert and Anne must have kept up their religious connections during this time because after living in Accrington for about ten years they moved to Preston. Robert was almost immediately elected President of the Mormon Church there. In fact it may be that he moved because he had been elected, but whichever came first he must have been attending the church at Preston and it is known that he had provided accommodation for visiting missionaries.

They didn't stay long in Preston. In less than two years they had decided to emigrate to America and go west to join the Mormons who were developing new settlements around what was to become Salt Lake City. They sailed from Liverpool in March 1856 aboard the *S.S. Enoch Train* and docked in Boston on April 30th. From there they travelled by train to New York and then on to Iowa City at the end of the Rock Island Line. The next 1200 miles had to be walked!

We assume, because of films and television, that all the pioneers went west in covered wagons, but the Mormon leader, Brigham Young, believed that handcarts would be quicker, cheaper and easier for immigrants to handle than teams of horses or oxen. So the Parker family loaded their belongings onto a handcart and joined the second group to make the trek, leaving Iowa City in June 1856 in a party of 221 people. Robert pulled, Maxi pushed, the others walked. Ada, the one year old who had been born in Preston, rode on the cart. The 1200 mile journey, including crossing the Rockies, took just less than four months, the party arriving at the Great Salt Lake at the end of September having lost just seven members during the trip.

Later in the year another party of emigrants made the same journey. Amongst them was a Scottish family named Gillies who had a nine year old daughter called Annie. On her twentieth birthday in July 1865 Annie married Maximilian Parker, who was then 21, in Beaver, Utah where they lived for several years and commenced a family which eventually totalled thirteen children. In 1879 Max bought a piece of land with a cabin near Circleville, growing crops and raising cattle. This became the family home and, because of its associations with Max's eldest son, is now a listed building of the State of Utah.

Robert LeRoy Parker, named after his grandfather, was born on Friday the thirteenth of April, 1866. He was thirteen when the family moved to Circleville where he spent his teens helping his father on the ranch, especially with the horses and cattle. By the time he was eighteen he had had various temporary jobs on other ranches, become friendly with some dubious characters and got involved on the fringes of cattle rustling. At 18 he left home to seek his fortune in the mining towns of Colorado but was soon in trouble accused of horse stealing. From then on he turned to a life of crime, specialising in bank robbery, safe-blowing and train hold-ups.

Robert Parker didn't operate alone. He was a member of a gang which included Bill Carver, Harvey Logan, Ben Kilpatrick and Harry Longabaugh. Their exploits have been immortalised and glamorised in books and films and they are as well-known as Jesse James, Billy the Kid or Wyatt Earp. But not under their own names, of course. Robert Parker is better known by his alias of *Butch Cassidy*. Harry Longabaugh called himself the *Sundance Kid* and the gang was known as *The Wild Bunch*. There are several conflicting theories about his eventual fate. Was he really killed in a shoot-out in South America or did he die of pneumonia at the age of 71 as his sister believed? But there is no doubt that *Butch Cassidy* missed being born in Accrington by quite a few years.

Bull Bridge in the latter years of the 19th century when it was the very centre of Old Accrington.

31

UNCLE ISAIAH

By Carole Hall

He didn't warrant my attention until I overhead someone relate that he'd pulled three teeth from his own head with pliers because they pained him, or so he said. That got me! At the first opportunity I dropped by after school, walking up Sultan Street, making a right along Water Street and found Aunt Minnie baking. She told me Uncle Isaiah was out back fixing a very rusty wheelbarrow. *"Hello there, young sprout, what brings you calling?"* he greeted me and I tried to peer at his mouth without being obvious but gushed instead, *"Is it true what they say then, Uncle?"* He looked across at me and I hurried to finish, *"That you took out your own teeth?"* I waited, a little thrilled, a little scared. *"Aye lass, that I did,"* he replied and my breath came out in a whistle. My estimation of my uncle shot up five points and I stared as if seeing him for the first time. *"There's brave you are!"* I declared and saw him smile. *"More convenience than bravery,"* he replied and motioned me close. *"There was a Great War in France, you know. In the trenches, we were, day in, day out, no doctors in that mud, so I took matters into my own hands, that's all."* *"I bet it hurt,"* I offered consolingly. *"Did they bleed much?"* Shaking his head he patted my shoulders, *"Not at all."* At that moment I was smitten with hero-worship for this tall son of Accrington whose soul was as sweet as the rain on the Coppice. He was 55 at the time and I was all of 11. I soon discovered he had wondrous tales to tell and thus made a practice of after-school visits. Among the stories was an account of his wedding day: *"Well, the big war's over now and here I am home from France. I asked your aunt if she'd have me, and we got ourselves married in Cambridge Street chapel..."* Aunt Minnie picked up the tale. *"There's handsome he was, you see! Your uncle all dressed in black broadcloth with a shirt as white as driven snow. And when the vows were said, and without so much as a by-your-leave from the preacher - I remember like it were yesterday - your uncle turned and sang 'The Rose of Tralee' just for me, and I said to myself, 'This man is all the gold and silver I'll ever need.'"* They smiled at each other in the remembering. I was just entering that soppy stage of pre-adolescence and thought it all so smashingly romantic, and believed my aunt the luckiest woman in the whole world, well in Accrington, any road. In those days, the Prudential rent man would come to each house to collect the monies, and Uncle Isaiah told me: *"Your Aunt Minnie was by far the prettiest girl in town and the Pru man got to flirting, so smitten he was with her bonny ways, but she said she'd have none of that! Well, he acted right daft and wouldn't be told, and one day I'm coming in the back door and see he's making a nuisance of himself again. 'If you can't hear, you'll have to feel!' I told him and sent the lad packing with a flea in his ear."* *"What did you do, Uncle?"* I asked, wide-eyed. He tossed his head back and laughed, remembering how it had been. *"Why I kicked his fancy bottom down the street for all the neighbours to see! Didn't have any more trouble from the likes of him. Daft bugger."* Aunt Minnie shushed him for swearing, but I thought it was a grand tale. Well the seasons slipped by and I grew tall. The years came and made the goodly couple old. One evening, after supper, Uncle Isaiah sat by the fire listening to the news on the wireless - as was his wont - and passed quietly, without fuss or bother, from this life to the next. I was proud to stand at his funeral, my hand warm in Aunt Minnie's, and I knew it would be a long time before I saw his like again. I keep his medals from the Great War in a plastic box, and an old soldier's cap I've had all these years. If I bury my nose deep inside I can smell him again.

JOSEPH BRIGGS AND HIS GIFT T0 THE TOWN

Atarah Hindle

The year 1932 became a milestone in the history of Accrington, for in the autumn of that year, the Corporation received a consignment of Tiffany glass, the gift of Joseph Briggs, an ex-Accrington lad, living in America. The world famous Tiffany Glass Studio in New York had closed its doors and ceased production, due to the decline in the market. A small town in Lancashire would be forever grateful...... In 1891, 17 year old Joseph Briggs left his home and family in Milnshaw Lane, and set sail for America. It had been his dream to go looking for the proverbial *'pot of gold'*. He was given three months leave of absence by his employers, but ended up staying there for 47 years!

When his family waved him off on his adventure, they could never have envisaged the successful career he would carve out for himself - as Louis Comfort Tiffany's right hand man! Prior to his employment as an apprenticed engraver at Steiner's Calico Printing Works, Church, his education consisted of attending Union Street Wesleyan Day School, and later the Mechanics Institute, where he studied science and art. Various tales are told of the ways in which Joseph raised the money for his fare. He had a performing goat and gave 'shows' to the local children, charging a few coppers. He also entertained with a 'Punch and Judy' show, and is reputed to have devised an alarm system for a local sweet shop, to stop youngsters taking sweets.

He spent his first night in New York, feeling terribly homesick, in a *'doss'* house. Here he met Seth Hathaway - a *'cowboy'* in a Buffalo Bill show. Joseph was startled to see all the other men in the room removing wooden legs, wigs, etc. They too were all part of some of the side-shows! Seth gave Joseph his first job - he had to hold objects out at arms length, whilst Seth attempted to shoot them out of his grasp! Joseph began looking elsewhere for employment, but he and Seth remained life-long pals. Seth was best man at Joseph's wedding, and once, whilst on a trip to England with his show, was known to have called on the Briggs' family in Milnshaw Lane.

Joseph had heard there may be work at the Tiffany Studio, so began to *'hang-around'*, hoping to secure employment. His persistence paid off, and he was given the job of brew-boy, beer-fetcher and spittoon emptier for the glassblowers. During his first few weeks at Tiffany's, Joseph took his lunch to work. This consisted of bread with sugar in-between. This saved him 5 cents. When he had accumulated about five dollars, he would send it home to his mother, assuring her that he had plenty of money to live on. There is not much information available regarding Joseph's rise to fame at the Tiffany Studios. During his spare time he designed and constructed mosaics from the glass discarded on the floor of the workshop. When this work came to the attention of Louis Comfort Tiffany, he was promoted to the mosaic department, and soon worked his way up to become foreman, then manager. He was responsible for some of the finest work ever carried out by the Tiffany Studios. (The famous Sulphur-Crested Cockatoo mosaic, on display at the Haworth Art Gallery, is attributed to being his own work) One of his children, Ruth, recalls that in the late 1920s, they were not actually sure the position their dad held. He was given different titles, being known as *'Manager'*, *'Art Director'* and *'Mr. Tiffany's Assistant'*.

It is not known how often Joseph returned to his home town, but he did so in 1901.

This was probably his last visit to England. He is believed to have been feeling homesick, and came to England with every intention of settling. He and his wife Elizabeth had sold all their belongings and given up their home. They stayed at the family home in Milnshaw Lane and intended going house hunting, but Joseph soon realized he would not be content in England, so returned to America. His proud parents arranged to have a memento of the visit, and so a formal family photograph captured the occasion. This was taken outside his parents home, *'Sunny Bank'*, Church. His father, Joseph Snr., was a foreman engraver at Steiner's. Joseph and his wife are at the right hand side of the photograph, holding their two young children Joseph Ashworth Briggs (who unfortunately died at a very early age) and Viola. They were to have four more children - Helen, Alice, Ruth and another son, whom they named Joseph Ashworth II.

Between the late 1880s and 1918, Tiffany products were at the height of fashion. They were created by Louis Comfort Tiffany and quickly became part of the *'Art Nouveau'* vogue. Production began in new furnaces at Corona, Long Island. It was here where the application and inclusion of metallic oxide in the firing of the glass to produce its unique iridescence was mastered. The glassware produced during this period ranks as some of the most technically brilliant work ever produced. Products ranged from glass tiles, leaded lamps, mosaics and vases, to stained glass windows and massive opal mosaic curtains for theatres. The beautiful mosaic and stained glass windows which Joseph was involved in were seen all over America. He was also involved in two very special memorial works. One was a window which he placed in a church, in memory of his first born son Joseph

Ashworth. The second memorial was dedicated to his mother. This was a large plaque with a bronze face with the Lord's Prayer on it in raised lettering. His daughter Ruth remembers one day going through the Ecclesiastical department at Tiffany's. An artist was working on a very large painting of Christ, with his hands outstretched. The artist told Joseph that he was having trouble getting the outstretched hand to look natural. Joseph took the artist's brush off him, and made a few sweeps of the arm and hand. Even Ruth could see a great improvement. She felt extremely proud of her modest dad that day!

After the First World War, views on art altered, and the superb work created at the Tiffany Studio was thought of as outmoded, and even repulsive! Tiffany did not like the new trends, and in 1924 he handed over the running of the company to Joseph Briggs. In 1928 Tiffany withdrew his financial support and the production of Tiffany glass ended. In the early 1930s, Joseph had the unpleasant task of trying to dispose of the company's remaining stock. Items that were once valued at more than 100 dollars failed to fetch more than 50c. In the summer of 1932 he had the foresight to ship three consignments of the glass back to Accrington. Approximately 140 pieces were presented to the Corporation of Accrington, and a similar amount were given to family and friends, the distribution being in the care of his family. Where are those pieces now? Most of them were probably thrown away years ago, although a Tiffany vase did turn up at TV's *'Antiques Road Show'* which visited Accrington in March 1995. The 1930s Town Council, although grateful for the gift, were more concerned with the Depression. At least one third of the townspeople were unemployed. The *'unfashionable'* glassware was thought of as being merely *'another exhibit for the museum'*. No-one had any idea that Joseph Briggs had given his town a priceless gift - *'an offering out of love and respect for the town of his birth'*. It was displayed in Oak Hill Museum on open shelves and window sills! When the Museum closed (1951) the glassware was transferred to the Haworth Art Gallery.

In 1958 the whole collection was valued at around £1500. *'Art Nouveau'* was being rediscovered, and its value began to increase. In 1964, and again in 1967, a gentleman enquired if Accrington Corporation would be prepared to sell the glass. It was decided not to sell. The Libraries and Art Gallery Committee went to view the collection and decided to retain the glassware. The Town had realized the importance of the gift, and declined to sell. The collection went on permanent display at the Haworth Art Gallery in January 1976. The 140 pieces, once left lying around on window sills, are now protected behind alarms and hardened glass. The lighting shows the glass to its best advantage.

Sixty years and more have elapsed since the generous donation of the Tiffany glassware to Accrington. It is recognised as one of the most important collections of Tiffany glass in the world. Joseph Ashworth Briggs II, who visited Accrington in 1992, added to the *'Tiffany Room'* by presenting an oil painting of his famous father, which now has pride of place there. Visitors cannot fail to be impressed by the glassware and by the love that Joseph Briggs had for his home town.

MEN OF MARK (& WOMEN TOO)

Many local lads and lasses have done well in life, leaving their mark in ways which bring honour to themselves and their town. I mention but a few of them:-

On the Board of Directors of Bass Brewery are a dozen men. Two of them are said to attend meetings wearing their Accrington Grammar School Old Boys ties. *Antony Portno* is a chemist with responsibility for beers. His father was *'Pug'*, a dearly-loved French master at the school. ✳✳✳✳✳✳ *Bryan Langton* was told by headmaster *'Ben'* Johnson that he would achieve little in life, so he left school instead of going to university to work in the hotel trade. He became head of their *'Holiday Inns'* group and was awarded a C.B.E. for his services to the Leisure industry. ✳✳✳✳✳✳ The signature of *Basil Gage Catterns* appeared on British banknotes between 1929 and 1934, whilst he was Chief Cashier of the Bank of England. His father was a vicar at St. Paul's, Oswaldtwistle, and Basil's first job was in the bank at the corner of Eagle Street and Cannon Street. ✳✳✳✳✳✳ *Doctor Reg Webster*, local Medical Officer of Health, became *'Brain of Britain'* in 1959. ✳✳✳✳✳✳ *James Drake*, another Grammar School lad, was knighted after he became Chief Surveyor and Bridgemaster to Lancashire County Council, and is credited with designing Britain's first stretch of motorway, near Preston, which opened in 1958 ✳✳✳✳✳✳ Another local lad to hold that office was *Harry Yeadon*, who gave his name to a stretch of road linking Blackpool to the M55, along the line of a former railway track. ✳✳✳✳✳✳ Achieving fame as one of *'The Liver Birds'*, actress *Polly James'* parents had an ice-cream business in Oswaldtwistle, where she was Pauline Devaney. In recent times, effervescent Polly opened Hyndburn's new Tourism Office in Accrington Town Hall. ✳✳✳✳✳✳ There had been locally-raised Members of Parliament for the Accrington (Hyndburn) Constituency before Ossie lad, *Ken Hargreaves*, threw his hat in the ring at the 1983 General Election as Conservative candidate, but none had won it by the narrow margin he achieved - just 21 votes, necessitating 5 recounts over 5 hours. At a celebration event held later in Ossie Town Hall, Ken won £4 in a bingo game. The other players demanded a recount. ✳✳✳✳✳✳ All-round athlete and P.E. teacher, *Val(erie) Robinson*, nee Walsh, took up hockey whilst a High School girl, and went on to become the *'first working-class girl'* to be capped for her country. Described as *'the world's best'*, she won 150 caps over a twenty year career (1964-84), and was awarded an O.B.E. for her services to the sport. ✳✳✳✳✳✳ Daughter of a Darwen librarian, *Joan Pomfret* continued to write under her maiden name when she married Accrington architect Douglas Townsend. A talented journalist, novelist and poet who deserves to have a book of her work compiled, Joan was a highly popular speaker on Lancashire literature and history - and a delightful person. In my view, she was the best female writer of Lancashire dialect material there has ever been. She died in 1993. ✳✳✳✳✳✳ Growing up with two brothers, a sister and musically-inclined parents, one of the first things young *Jon Anderson* did as a 1960s teenager was to follow his brother, Tony, into 'The Warriors' pop group, then taking East Lancashire by storm. He went on to found 'YES', one of the world's leading and long-lasting rock bands. He has composed and sung countless top-selling hits, his most successful one being *'Wondrous Stories'* which he wrote and performed with 'YES' as a top-ten entry in the late 1970s. He is famed too for his association with, amongst others, Demis Roussos and Vangelis. The theme song for the hit film *'Chariots of Fire'* had music by Vangelis and words by Jon. He has enjoyed a highly successful solo career. ✳✳✳✳✳✳ Another local singer who rose from humble beginnings, singing in an Ossie Methodist chapel choir and with the Accrington Male Voice Choir to international recognition as an opera singer is **John Tomlinson**. At the Grammar School he declined to take 'O-level' music, preferring (though there was a hit of rebellion) the scientific subjects which were to lead to a civil engineering degree at Manchester University. The opening paragraph of 'The Sunday Express' music page on 10th October 1993 reads: *'John Tomlinson, the mighty British bass-baritone crowned his reputation as one of the world's leading singers at Covent Garden last week'*. Enough said. ✳✳✳✳✳✳ Probably the first *'star'* to emerge from Accrington was John Stevens Oldham, known professionally as **Derek Oldham**. He rose from being a member of Accrington Amateurs, whilst still at Grammar School, to sing in theatres in London and America. He recorded over eighty times for HMV as a member of the D'Oyly Carte Opera Company, and appeared in films as a straight actor. In the First World War, he won the Military Cross. He had joined the Scots Guards as a private but became a commissioned officer in the East Lancs Regiment. ✳✳✳✳✳✳ Born in Huncoat in 1934, and educated at St. John's and the Grammar School, young **Harrison Birtwistle** was a *'somewhat unruly boy'* who has achieved international recognition as a music composer in the classical and operatic fields. He owes it all to his mother, who bought him a clarinet, paid for lessons and got him to join a local military band. He has been described as *'the most famous unknown composer in the history of music'*. He was knighted in 1988. ✳✳✳✳✳✳✳ Mauve-loving **Benita Moore** was born (as Benita Houston) and bred in Church and has become a locally and nationally-known figure through her presentation of Lancashire working-class life in books. Mostly they record her interviews with old folk keen to tell their memories, though she tells a good tale herself, both in prose and rhyme - but what else would you expect from someone who has worked as a librarian locally since 1955? Benita's best work has yet to come - she plans to write about her Church childhood. ✳✳✳✳✳✳ In 1985, at the age of 25 years, **Jeanette Winterson** won the coveted Whitbread First Novel Prize with *'Oranges are not the only fruit'*. Since then she has risen to the very top of the British literary scene, and is as outspoken, rebellious and opinionated as any literary figure ever was. She proclaims her sexual preferences and has spoken openly about her Accrington childhood in a strict religious household. It should not surprise anyone if, in the near future, parties of (mostly) women are seen being conducted on a tour of 'Winterson's Accrington', keen to learn where their heroine spent her childhood. ✳✳✳✳✳✳ Several local lads have become *'first citizens'* of other towns. **John Harwood**, born in 1832 to a lowly Ossie family, worked as a *'tearer'* at Foxhill Bank Print Works before, seeking to improve himself, setting off for Manchester. For a while, he drove a stage coach between there and Rochdale, then took work as a painter and decorator, becoming a partner in the firm. A knighthood and the office of Lord Mayor of Manchester followed. ✳✳✳✳✳✳ **Riley Lord** was born six years after John Harwood, in cottage property which got knocked down so that the Manchester Road/Grange Lane Fire Station could be built. His life story reads like a chapter from Smiles' book *'Self Help'*. Through his own endeavours he became a *'Man from the Pru'* (an agent for the Prudential Assurance Company) in the North-East, Lord Mayor of Newcastle and a knight of the realm in 1900. ✳✳✳✳✳✳ **Harold Davenport** certainly did his sums right. Born in Accrington in 1907, he went on from the Grammar School to become a Fellow of Trinity College, Cambridge and, without a shadow of doubt, one of the top mathematicians in the world. ✳✳✳✳✳✳ Born in New Zealand,

Oliver Vaughan Snell Bulleid, (O.V.S. to his friends) came to live in Ossie where his relative William Sanderson was an accountant, Colonel of the East Lancashire Royal Horse Artillery and a keen swordsman. He was definitely *'middle-class'* and worked to keep young Oliver away from the influences of Lancashire speech he encountered at the recently opened Accrington Technical School. One of the first pupils, Bulleid excelled there and went on to become one of the finest railway engineers the world has known. *'The last giant of steam'*, he held posts as Chief Engineer of the Southern Railway, Southern Region of British Railways and was President of umpteen Institutes. A Lt.-Colonel in the First World War, he died in 1970. ✳✳✳✳✳✳ The name of *James Brown Whittaker* means nowt to our nation. He was a lad brought up in Church and Clayton, attended the Grammar School (where he was 'Jimmy Wick') before becoming a teacher at Hyndburn Park School, then quitting the classroom for the world of entertainment as *Jim Bowen*, comedian and famed host of *'Bullseye'*, a darts-based TV programme, and a super, smashing, great, down-to-earth Lancashire lad. Read his autobiography *'From a Bundle of Rags'*. ✳✳✳✳✳✳ In the same class as Jim, but truly in a class of his own, is an athlete who might easily have been called *'Run'* instead of *Ron Hill*, for that is what he has been doing since the days he became Accrington Grammar School, then Lancashire Schools, then British Cross-Country champion. Ron gained a doctorate in textile chemistry at Manchester University, so followed in a very long and distinguished Accrington lineage. He competed in three Olympic Games (1964, 1968 & 1972) at long-distance events, became both European and Commonwealth Marathon Champion, and in 1970 was the first Briton to win the Boston Marathon. After a spell with Bolton Harriers, Ron returned to the fold of Clayton Harriers in 1976. Now in business selling his own brand of sportswear, Ron is still up and running every day - and has done so every day without exception for over thirty years. He has run in 57 different countries - not bad for a lad who was inspired to run in the first place by the exploits of Alf Tupper, hero of *'The Rover'* (or maybe it was *'The Adventure'* or *'Wizard'*), who trained for his running by eating fish and chips. Ron restricts himself to eating them only every Thursday. Make no mistake - Ron Hill is in the same line-up as Bannister, Chattaway, Coe, Ovett, Christie, Daley Thompson…and Alf Tupper. Read his autobiography, which comes in two parts - *'The Long Hard Run'*. ✳✳✳✳✳✳ Running behind Ron by a few years, *David Lewis* may have trained on Holland's pies, as he worked there for a while after a spell in Accrington Library. A Physical Education degree up his sleeve, David has run in an England vest many times at many (long) distances and, as I write, has become English Cross-Country Champion for the third time, ✳✳✳✳✳✳ Another who served his country, though not in the top job in his profession, was *Robert Wade*, a native of our town who, in 1895, became a public hangman's assistant. By this time, he was living in Bolton, where lived several hangmen. He trained at Newgate Prison. There is no record of him in action after November 1895, though he was still 'on the list' in 1901. ✳✳✳✳✳✳ You wouldn't expect to find a composer and publisher of music in Back Lane, Baxenden, but in the 1930s, at No.28, lived *Fred Hodgson*, whose professional name was T. Leston-Parrs. His name appears on many sheet music copies which, when closely examined, show his address as Bach Lane. ✳✳✳✳✳✳ In the 'Swinging Sixties', the name of *Ossie Clark* was prominent in the popular fashion world of 'Carnaby Street', the 'Tin Pan Alley' of the rag trade. This garment guru, designer of dresses for dolly birds and debutantes, is really called Raymond, but chose to call himself after the town where he spent his childhood - and it did him no harm. Consider what might have been the case if he had called himself *'Gobbin Clark'*. ✳✳✳✳✳✳ Promotion doesn't come much higher than Church of England Bishop, which was achieved by Ossie lad **Herbert Bury**, who was Bishop of British Honduras, then Bishop of Northern & Central Europe for fifteen years, which included the First World War. He died in 1933. Prior to being a churchman he had a spell as a cattle rancher in Argentina. ✳✳✳✳✳✳ During the Second World War, Claytonian **Daniel Ellwood** worked as an Intelligence Officer. This was quite a change from his peacetime job with Blackburn Corporation Transport Department. One day, searching a house, he found a recently-issued German passport belonging to one James Joyce, the infamous 'Lord Haw-Haw'. In it, Joyce was described as being an *'Englander'*, and because of this, it could be proved that he was capable of committing treason against his country. He was *'seen off'*, and all through the keen observation of a man who was to become Chairman of Clayton-le-Moors Co-op. ✳✳✳✳✳✳ There's another Accrington connection with Joyce's trial. Another of the witnesses was Detective Superintendent **John Woodmansey**, in charge of alien records at Police Headquarters, Hutton. He later became Chief Superintendent in charge of Accrington Division. I learned of this connection in the very last days of researching before hitting my deadline when I picked up a book at a Secondhand Book Fair. ✳✳✳✳✳✳ In 1930, the marvellous book *'Accrington Captains of Industry'* was published. That was too early to include **William Wiggins Cocker**. Raised in Buxton Street, he sold papers behind the Market Hall as a lad, and worked for a Church grocer before getting a job with a manufacturing chemist. He set up in a room in Infant Street in the 1930s making paint, aided by his cousin Wesley Cocker (later Professor). That was the start for a man who was to become a major employer in the town, with a factory the first to make D.D.T. on a big scale. Mayor, County Councillor, Freeman of the Borough, he was knighted for his services to Lancashire. Truly a captain of industry. ✳✳✳✳✳✳ Green Haworth Methodist Chapel was the training ground for an Ossie lad who described his boyhood as *'work, bed and Sundays at Chapel'*. God called **Jimmy Butterworth** away from the drudgery of Steiner's and newspaper selling when he was 17 years old, in 1917. His first posting was to a chapel in Camberwell, S.E.London - and there he stayed for 54 years. His name is written in capital letters in the annals of the Methodist Church as being the founder, with just six lads in one room, of what became known as *'Clubland'*, a club where London's youth could go to take them off the crime-ridden streets and be helped towards a better life. ✳✳✳✳✳✳ Another top man in his chosen field was **Leo Cheney** (1883-1928), who worked at the same bank as did Basil Catterns, mentioned earlier. Always a talented artist, he left Accrington to pursue a career as a newspaper artist, becoming one of the finest cartoonists in the country. His most famous commercial work was his designing of a whisky-drinking *'Johnny Walker'*. ✳✳✳✳✳✳ Artists are popularly perceived to be eccentric, flamboyant, often larger-than-life (unless they starved in a garret). All these words describe **Gerard Henriques de Rose** (-1987) of whom it was said *"There is no question that his paintings stand with the greatest portrait painters, Valasquez, Hals and Van Dyke"*. The commentator wet on to say *"An artist of his calibre must have a free spirit of the same order and the fact that he possesses such a spirit can be seen not only in his work but in his life and personality"*. He hit the nail on the head, for Gerry was a character who became a New Orleans-based, internationally famous artist of the rich and famous. Stars, Nobility and artists, as well as the residents of Dallas commissioned him. Born in Oxford Street of a Franco-Russian father and Accrington

Mother, he never forgot his home town and returned to it, to the delight of all his friends, who recall him, his slight stammer and flamboyance, with affection. He was once locked up for driving whilst drunk, but got off because the magistrates realised that what the police had seen as extraordinary behaviour was Gerry's ordinary demeanour. I have no photograph of Gerry to show readers, but he has been described as *"a dead ringer for Charlie Drake"*, who happened to be a friend of his. ✳✳✳✳✳✳ Moor End School and the Grammar School fitted **Kenneth Barnes** (b. 1922) for a place at Balliol College, Oxford, a wartime spell with the Lancashire Fusiliers and then a career in the Civil Service. He rose to what has become known, because of the TV series *'Yes Minister'*, as a *'Sir Humphrey'* to four Ministers of Employment. Officially this position is 'Permanent Secretary'. Knighted for his services to the country, this son of a Church *'scrap metal chap'* has had a good woman behind him in the form of Barbara, nee Ainsworth, also a Grammar School student, who has had a career in Surrey politics. ✳✳✳✳✳✳ Perhaps the best known local footballer was **Jack Bray**, born in Ossie in 1909, who cost Manchester City £1,000 in 1929. He played for them 257 times, and gained 10 England caps. Later, managing Watford, he was a local hero, but he never forgot his days with St. Andrew's, Ossie and Clayton Olympia. His brother, **George Bray**, was a top player too, who joined Burnley from Great Harwood in 1937. The war interrupted his career and perhaps denied him international honours. He is remembered as *'a hard tackling half-back who never gave less than 100%'*. Even after his playing days, George was devoted to Burnley F.C., though another member of the family, **John Bray**, played for Blackburn Rovers in the early 1960s. ✳✳✳✳✳✳ **Robert Trotter Hermon-Hodge** was Accrington's M.P. from 1886 to 1892. Although he was then defeated by a Liberal, he was a great favourite in the town, being known as *'Our Hermon'*, and many lads christened Herman were named after him. He went on to represent other constituencies, but didn't forget his ties with the town, and when he was created baron in 1919, he chose the name *'Baron Wyfold* (the name of his house in Reading) *of Accrington'*. The third baron sits in the Lords today, but sadly has no heir, so the title will die. ✳✳✳✳✳✳ Born in Ossie in 1901, **Eddie Paynter** worked in a brickworks as a lad and lost the ends of two fingers in an accident there. Luckily, he was a left-hander and these were off his right hand. His father was an Enfield player, and so was Eddie. He joined Lancashire C.C.C. in 1926 but didn't get a regular first team place until 1930. He became an England player in 1931, but it was on the 1932/33 tour of Australia that he achieved immortal fame when playing in the Brisbane Test. After two days play, he was rushed to hospital with acute tonsilities and high temperature. After a Sunday break, play resumed on Monday, the third day, and Eddie heard England's wickets tumbling on his bedside radio, so stole out of hospital in his dressing gown and pyjamas, and took a taxi to the ground. There, his offer to bat was accepted, and he stayed at the crease for over an hour as *'nightwatchman'*. Another night in hospital, then back to the crease to take his score to 83 to give England the first innings lead. In the second innings, when Eddie took up his willow, it was his *'sixer'* which won the match. Arriving back home, he received a hero's welcome, but it didn't turn the head of this people's fighting cock. He never lost touch with Clayton and Enfield. As heroes go, Eddie is in England's first eleven. He *'went to the pavilion'* in 1979. ✳✳✳✳✳✳ **Jack Simmons**, known as *'Flat Jack'* because of his bowling style, was born in Clayton in 1941. He didn't make the England Test team, but is up there with the best of cricketers. Jack's father and grandfather played for Enfield, so he naturally followed, getting into the first team at fourteen years of age, when Clyde Walcott (now there was a giant) was professional. Jack went on to 'pro' with Baxenden before joining Lancashire when he was 27 years old. In 1984, Jack was one of five named *'Cricketer of the Year'* by Wisden. Perhaps his greatest achievement was in guiding'Tasmania to becoming Australian one-day champions. His reputation there is so high he is regarded as *'King of Tasmania'*. Here, he has to make do with an M.B.E. ✳✳✳✳✳✳ Straight from Rhyddings School to Lancashire County Cricket Club went 15 year old *David Lloyd*. He was already playing for Accrington, and was perhaps the first Lancashire League associate to captain the county. *'Bumble's'* career figures for appearances and runs for Lancashire (1965-83) and England (9 Tests) are impressive - 19,269 runs, 237 wickets, 334 catches. He went on to 'pro' for Accrington, coach at Old Trafford and become a commentator on the game worth listening to. His lad, Graham Lloyd, followed in his father's footsteps. David is a fine ambassador for Accrington. After all, *'You can take a lad out of Accy, but you can't take Accy out of a lad'*. ✳✳✳✳✳✳ *Graeme 'Foxy' Fowler*, *'a Lancastrian through and through'*, was born in 1957 and attended the Grammar School. He was the youngest opening bat in the Lancashire League, just 15 years old, and that is only one of several records he was to achieve playing for Lancashire (233 games, 1979-92) and England. He is the only batsman to have scored a century in both innings of a first class match with the aid of a runner, and the first Englishman to score a double century against India in India. ✳✳✳✳✳✳ Burnley born (in 1941), *Tom Sisson* had the sense to marry an Ossie girl and settle down there in the early '60s whilst a collier at Thorny Bank Pit, Hapton. Without formal training, he took an interest in art and mastered the silk screen method of printmaking. He has exhibited his black and white images in galleries on the continent, in Canada, and in 1993 he took 200 of his prints to exhibit in China - for the second time. He has shown his work at the Royal Academy, London, and elsewhere in this country. Much of his work has a strong local history theme. He is influenced by his days in t'pit and by his surroundings. Recently asked to produce a Christmas card for Hyndburn M.P., Greg Pope, Tom chose the railway viaduct, overlooked by the Pendle Hill he saw as a lad. ✳✳✳✳✳✳ Many cricketers are known for their prowess with bat and ball, but few *'stumpers'* achieve such high recognition. Matchwinner *Richard Pilling* (1855-91) was known as *'The Prince of English Wicketkeepers'*. He came to live in Church when nobbut a lad, and joined the *'West Enders'* when 19 years old. He played for Lancashire 177 times (1877-89) and for England 8 times (1887/8). Following a football match about 1890, he contracted inflammation of the lungs and this ended his cricket career. Lancashire C.C.C. sent him to Australia to recuperate over the winter but he died six days after returning home. ✳✳✳✳✳✳ *John Blake* died in 1900 aged 64 years. Of Irish descent and a native of Stockport. He was a prolific inventor from the age of 18 years and came from Stockport to work at Christie's Foundry, on the site of the Market Hall. After a short spell as a partner, he set up on his own in Oxford Street. His international reputation as an inventor, engineer and manufacturer grew when he started to produce a self-acting pump which needed minimal attention. *'Blake's Hydraulic Ram'* could raise huge amounts of water great distances. His company, which went public in 1897, supplied pumps around the world, including the Indian Government for use in the water fountains of the Taj Mahal. His company is today part of the Allspeeds Group based in Clayton, and still supplies water pumps to the world. ✳✳✳✳✳✳ Looking upwards rather than *'down in the mouth'* brought dentist *Geoff Garnett*, another Grammar School product, from the Ossie surgery he shares with his wife to the *'top job'* (Chairman) of the British Dental Association. It is regarded as highly unusual in dental circles for an *'ordinary'* dentist, as opposed to one operating in academic surroundings, to reach such a position. Geoff was appointed a magistrate but had to resign through pressure of business. ✳✳✳✳✳✳ **Kenneth Ball's** father ran a carpet business in Bridge Street. After leaving the Grammar School, Ken left Accrington for Brighton, and as a 27 year old in 1956, he started to sell motoring books in a part time way, later developing into publishing *'Autobooks'*. The success was immediate, and resulted in him selling the copyright and his company for £1.3 million. Perhaps his secret was in marrying a Huncoat lass, Mary Philips, in the first place. He is now a consultant on pre-1940 motor cars and dealer in rare car books. ✳✳✳✳✳✳ Many students of Accrington Art School have gone on to achieve success in their field of artistic pursuit, but few have done it through their skill with clay. **Derek Emms** (born 1929) studied at the Grammar School before going to the Art School, then on through a famous pottery to become a teacher at Stoke Art College. Now retired, he enjoys a national reputation as a studio potter specialising in making tea pots and with his use of glazes. He works in stoneware and porcelain. The Haworth Art Gallery and Townley Hall have examples of his work. ✳✳✳✳✳✳ Arriving by stagecoach from Warwickshire in 1841, **Henry Dunckley** entered the Accrington Baptist College as one of its six pupils. His diligence earned him a scholarship award for Glasgow University, where he gained an M.A. degree. He became a Baptist minister in Salford, always keeping strong links with his Accrington friends, and was a prize-winning essayist as well as finding time to be a current affairs commentator for the Liberal newspaper *The Manchester Examiner & Times*. In 1854 he resigned his ministry to take over the editor's desk at that paper. He took on the pen-name **'Verax'** and revealed a prophetic strain in everything he wrote, the Press being his pulpit. He was held in very high regard in Manchester and the North. He died in 1896. ✳✳✳✳✳✳ From a job working with clay and terra-cotta at the brickworks, **Walter Marsden** went to Accrington School of Art & Crafts. After a spell as a captain in the Army under Lord Kitchener's influence and eye, he became a teacher and highly respected sculptor on the international scene. His skill as designer and executor can still be seen on the War Memorials in Gatty Park, in Bolton and in St. Annes on Sea. He died aged 86 in 1969. ✳✳✳✳✳✳ Very few, if any, local solicitors have become full time circuit judges, but one who is in that category is **Edward Slinger**. His appointment in 1995 was unusual in that he was a solicitor and not a barrister. Edward went from the Grammar School (where he ran with Ron Hill) to practise locally. He practised at the nets too, and was good enough to captain Enfield and Lancashire Second XI. He comes from a family associated with the law and the meat trade.

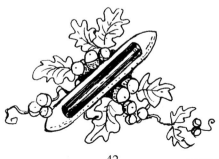

CHRISTOPHER WHITTAKER & COMPANY LTD.
Its Founders and Early History
Martin J. Crossley Evans

The liquidation in 1972 of Christopher Whittaker and Company Ltd., Dowry Street, brought to an end a firm founded 118 years earlier by brothers Christopher and Thomas Whittaker. Their brick-making machinery was recognised as being the most efficient of its kind and was exported to all parts of the world. Alderman Thomas Whittaker (1833-1902) was described by a contemporary as a man who had *"raised himself from a very humble position to occupy a foremost place in the town"*. The sons of an illiterate labouring man, Thomas and his eldest brother, Christopher (1815-1865), obtained a rudimentary education. While working as mechanics at the Sunnyside and Broad Oak print works, they invented a machine for washing calico, which allowed the three processes of printing, dyeing and finishing to be executed continuously. Calico pieces were sewn together, fed into the machinery, and detached at the end of the process. The machine was developed when Thomas was aged twenty-one. With his brother, he obtained financial support from Joseph Duxbury. Together they obtained a patent for the Continuous Calico Washing Machine and in 1854 founded Christopher Whittaker and Company. Thomas was the commercial traveller of the firm, and built up a series of clients who helped the company to widen the scope of its business as engineers, millwrights, and iron and brass founders. The machine became popular with mill owners because it saved time and manpower, but it was resented by the workforces of the mills into which it was introduced.

In 1872, the company acquired James Matthews' patent for semi-dry brick making machinery. The patent was purchased with the help of John Clayton, a Burnley tobacconist, whose financial interest was subsequently purchased by the firm. The brick making machinery was designed to manufacture bricks from ground clay, fed from the mill to the machine via a riddle and elevator. The clay was subjected to great pressure, formed into blocks, and delivered at the front of the machine in readiness for walling in a kiln. The process took ten minutes from the extraction of the clay to walling in the kiln ready for firing. The machine could be operated by a boy. Two men extracting clay, one filling the mill pan, and the boy made up a small, economical workforce. The machine produced 14 bricks per minute, or 840 per hour, and could be used for forming blocks of cement of any size or shape by the insertion into the machine of Whittaker's patented expanding mould.

Gradually the company's textile interests were phased out as the brick-making and refractory parts of the business expanded. By the end of the century the manufacture of brick making machinery and the engines to drive it had become the most profitable part of the business. American patents were obtained in 1884, 1890, 1896 and 1902. In the mid-1890s Whittakers acquired Messrs. Furnevall and Company, textile plant manufacturers specialising in machinery for the finishing trade, with their Union Foundry at Haslingden. By the time that C. Whittaker and Company was turned into a private Limited Company (1897) it was exporting machinery to South Africa, the Far East, the United States of America, New Zealand, France, Italy and Russia. It had expanded its business into the field of sanitary engineering, manufacturing such products as the patent Acme sanitary pipe. The company also made machinery for a variety of associated industries; refractories for the manufacture of kilns, fire bricks and crucibles; and machinery to form drain pipes and tiles. By 1900 the

The invalid Accrington poetess, Janie Whittaker, flanked by her parents, Alderman and Mrs. Whittaker, at the bottom of the steps to their family homw, 'Sunnyside House', 141, Burnley Road, about 1895. *(Accrington Library Local History Collection)*

name Whittaker was recognised and respected in all parts of the world where there were extensive clay working industries. The firm established agencies in places as diverse as South Africa and New Zealand, and continued to expand until the outbreak of the Great War. As the company expanded and prospered, Thomas Whittaker and his sons, Christopher, Thomas junior, and Laurence decided to form a new firm, and sold the patents of the old company to the newly formed Christopher Whittaker and Company (1900) Ltd. in return for a financial interest in the new company and a large cash payment.

Between 1878 and 1918, the Whittaker family played an important role in the town. Accrington gained a charter and became a borough in 1878. Thomas Whittaker began his public career in the same year, when he was elected a councillor. He was elected an alderman in 1886, became Chairman of the General Works Committee in 1888, served as mayor between 1890 and 1893, and was appointed a magistrate in 1892. A Liberal in national politics, a friend of the poor and an advocate of Old Age Pensions, he was a committed Wesleyan, and served as a Sunday school teacher for many years.

On the death of Alderman Thomas Whittaker in 1902, his eldest surviving son, Christopher junior (1859-1918) succeeded as the Chairman. The Alderman's other sons, Thomas junior (1861-1938) and Laurence (1869-1948), who had both spent the whole of their business careers in the firm, became joint managing directors.

Christopher junior, a qualified analytical chemist, entered the chemical industry on the death of his father-in-law in the 1880s, and took charge of the Globe Chemical Works, Church, which later merged with the United Indigo and Chemical Company, of which he became chairman. He was a pioneer of the treatment of sewage by bacteria, and in 1898-

44

1899 formed the Automatic Sewerage Distributors Ltd. at Church, to manufacture and to market his newly patented sewage treatment machinery. While on the town council (1891-1900), Christopher was chairman of the joint sewerage board, contributing to their deliberations his extensive knowledge both of heavy sanitary wares and of the most up-to-date treatment methods.

During the Great War, Thomas junior was increasingly left to shoulder the full burden of running C. Whittaker and Company Ltd. By 1915, his elder brother, Christopher junior, was in poor health and until his death in July. 1918, Christopher devoted his energies to the war effort. Christopher's two sons by his first marriage, Captains Norman and Hugh Allen Whittaker were on active service in France. Laurence, at the age of 46, had left the firm to accept a commission in the R.A.M.C. He became the Captain-Quartermaster of Tidworth Military Hospital, near Salisbury. At the end of the war his work was recognised by Lloyd George's government in the New Year's honours list for 1919 by the award of one of the country's first MBEs. On his de-mobilisation, he resigned from the firm and settled in Frome, Somerset, in 1920.

In 1919, Norman, Christopher's eldest son, returned from the war, and a power struggle developed between him and Thomas junior. During 1919-1920, Thomas junior left the company and with two of his three sons established Thomas Whittaker and Sons at Canal Foundry, Church. The resultant battle between the two companies was bitterly contested. In the edition of The Clayworker for August 1920 the new firm, using the trade name and the trade description of the machinery produced by the more established company, attempted to poach business from Christopher Whittaker and Company. Misleading advertising, infringement of patents, the canvassing of customers of the old firm and extensive use of information .gained by Thomas junior when he was managing director of the elder company led the new company to the law courts and ultimately to bankruptcy. By 1922 *'Mr. Norman'* was left in undisputed possession of his grandfather's firm, their old clients, and the patents, to carry the firm's high standards of engineering into a new era.

Editor's Note:-A new era was perhaps in the mind of *'Mr. Norman'* from 1922 onwards. We know for certain that in 1911 the company's machines bore the name *'New Era'*, for about 1950, the firm started up its own football team to play in the local league - The New Era Football Club. A lad called Michael (?) Barrett and myself, when dressed in the team's gold and black strip with N.E. badge, were its keenest followers. Our fathers worked at *'Whicks'* and I lived in its shadow in Dowry Street. The firm's telegraphic address was *'Bricks!'*

HYNDBURN AND THE RISE OF BRITISH CHEMISTRY
Frank Dewhurst

East Lancashire became associated with the rise of the chemical and dyeing Industries in the late 1760s when the father of Sir Robert Peel started printing at Brookside, between Accrington and Blackburn. By 1772 the Peels and their partners had commenced printing at Church Bank, near Church Kirk. From these works we may "trace the origin of the extensive print works of Lancashire, which for their magnitude and efficiency are not surpassed, if equalled, by any in Europe" (London Journal of Design and Manufactures, 1850) In particular works at Primrose (Clitheroe), Sabden, Oakenshaw (Clayton) and Broad Oak: (Accrington) were established. The Broad Oak works, set up in 1792 under the firm of Fort, Taylor and Bury prospered and when the Journal of Design and Manufactures ran a series of papers on "the Rise and Progress of the great Manufacturies of this Kingdom" they had "great pleasure in commencing the series with a manufactory so eminent as Messrs. Hargreaves' Print Works at Broad Oak, Accrington".

It was at the same factory in 1941 that Rex Whinfield and J.T.Dickson discovered Terylene and gave birth to the Polyester Industry. This industry developed world wide, but key work on the difficult problems of dyeing these novel fibres was carried out at the Broad Oak Works.

John Mercer, the greatest local chemist

Edward Frankland described a trip to East Lancashire during 1847 when *"the most interesting incident......was my making the acquaintance of Mr. John Mercer, at Oakenshaw, for he was, perhaps, one of the most clever and interesting men I have ever met with"*. Frankland, one of the leading British chemists of the mid-to-late Victorian period, knew all the leading British and German scientists of that time. Mercer was clearly a most remarkable man to stand out amongst such company. He was born in 1791 in Great Harwood, observing later in life that in his estimation no earthly spot was more beautiful. The family had been hard hit by the famine following the 1799 crop failure and he recalled as a nine year old going *"up and down seeking docks, which my mother boiled for us to make a meal"*. He began work at nine as a bobbin minder and his father died in the epidemic which followed the famine. He received his first instruction in reading, writing and arithmetic at the age of ten when a pattern designer, named Blenkinsop, from Oakenshaw Print Works recognised his abilities and offered to give him lessons in the evenings. Mercer was extremely gifted and was able to continue to educate himself after Blenkinsop moved. In 1807 his mother remarried and the young Mercer *"was all on fire to learn dyeing"* after seeing a beautiful orange coloured dress his baby stepbrother was wearing. He had no books nor recipes for dyeing and no dyers lived near his home. He knew there were fancy dyers in Blackburn and discovered they got their materials from a local pharmacy. Mercer did not know what he wanted, but asked the shopman what sort of things he sold the dyers. On hearing they bought peachwood, brazilwood, logwood, quercitron, alum, copperas and others he reckoned up his money, found he could afford three pennyworth of each, and set to work with the energy, perseverance, careful observation and systematic experimentation which was natural to him, making a name for himself locally in dyeing in a small way and was taken on in 1809 as an apprentice at the Oakenshaw Print Works but encountered obstruction from a jealous old foreman. Trade was badly affected by the Napoleonic Wars in 1810, and the

Oakenshaw Works had to let their apprentices go. He returned to handloom weaving for a living, and occupied his leisure with music and mathematics, which he taught himself. About this time Mercer met John Lightfoot, the father of the family of local textile chemists of that name. Lightfoot was the local excise man responsible for assessing the quality of printed calico, which was subject to a duty of three pence a yard, when produced at the local printworks.

Lightfoot, being well educated with a knowledge of mathematics, the physical sciences and some chemistry, assisted Mercer in his studies. Mercer was always grateful to him, and valued both his help and friendship all his life.

By 1813, Mercer was buying cheaply from the dyeworks *'spent'* material from which he was able to extract useful dyes. Benjamin Hargreaves of Broad Oak observed that *"Much waste of valuable colouring-matter frequently took place, and instances are remembered where fifty or a hundred pounds worth of spoiled colour was thrown into the nearest brook, which in the hands of an economical chemist, would have been turned to a profitable account."* Parkinson's Chemical Pocket-book, which he bought in 1814 at a bookstall in Blackburn market on the day he bought his marriage licence, was his first chemistry textbook.

In his own words *"It introduced me into a new world. I devoured it"*. By 1817, using the book as a basis, he made his first major contribution to textile chemistry when he discovered Antimony Orange. In 1818 he began work at the Oakenshaw Print Works, and never looked back. More on Mercer later.

Some Other Local Chemists

According to Mercer, in 1818, the Thomsons at Clitheroe and the Hargreaves at Accrington were the only printing firms in the country employing a man with a knowledge of chemistry. James Thomson, an associate of Humphrey Davey, had studied chemistry at Glasgow. Thomas Hargreaves (1771-1822) had learned printing at Sabden, but in 1817 he had brought over Frederick Steiner, an established textile chemist from Alsace. Steiner moved to Thomson in 1821, recommending John Emmanuel Lightfoot as his successor at Broad Oak. Steiner moved back to Church in 1824, and set up on his own in 1836. He made significant advances both in the use of sodium stannate and in the Turkey Red area.

The Lightfoot and Hargreaves families provided a series of able chemists for the Broad Oak works. Several of the Hargreaves sons were educated at Glasgow University on the recommendation of Thomson, and also worked in Dalton's laboratory in Manchester: whilst Benjamin Hargreaves (1806-1880) went to Edinburgh University after working under Dalton. Lawrence Hargreaves was regarded as unusually able, but died young of typhoid in 1822. His father never got over this and died soon afterwards. The Lightfoots learned their textile chemistry at Broad Oak, although Lightfoot Senior, the exciseman, certainly would have tutored them as he did the Hargreaves boys. Whilst not a chemist, he made a good tutor. The value of a sound education for the young and an inspiring teacher, is easily overlooked, but Mercer always acknowledged his gratitude to Lightfoot Senior. They both knew that *'industry and prudence conquer'*. The Hargreaves and Lightfoots made solid contributions to printing technology, but John Lightfoot (1832-72) was probably the best chemist, and is famous for his discovery of Aniline Black. His careful and well thought out work in developing his colour style was notable, but his work using camphor to detect grease contamination of water showed him to have a very sharp chemical brain and a sound grasp of the subject.

The Glasgow and Manchester-educated William Blythe (1813-79) was another able chemist, who started work in Church in 1835. He had patents with Mercer, with John Dyneley Prince from America on fabric preparation, and with Emile Kopp of Accrington on improvements in soda ash and sulphuric acid manufacture.

Frederik Albert Gatty (1819-88) was brought from Alsace by Steiner in 1842 and set up independently in 1843. His Turkey Red-Garancin, *'Gatty Red'* was notable, but he was most famous for his discovery of the lightfast Khaki dye.

The greatest local chemist was John Mercer, who went beyond laying the foundations of textile chemistry to make contributions to chemistry as a whole. It is impossible to do him justice in a few words. He developed the use of inorganic pigments in printing fabrics, extending his early Antimony Orange to Manganese Brown, after seeing manganese slip being used at Broadfield Pottery, near Green Haworth. He pioneered the use of arsenates and phosphates to replace cow dung, chromates as dyes and oxidising agents, and developed a wide range of oxidising and reducing agents. He extended the use of lead and tin compounds, and added to the knowledge of tin chemistry. He developed methods for standardising bleach, and for water analysis. He made significant advances in solution chemistry, in the area of vegetable dyes such as indigo, madder, garancin, cochineal and catechu and in the formation of lakes; (coloured compounds resulting from colouring agents and alumina compounds). His production of "sulphated oil" for the Turkey Red process was another major advance.

His discovery of *'Mercerisation'*, (the modification of cotton to produce artificial silk) and his discovery of the solubility of cellulose in ammoniacal copper solutions laid the foundations of the rayon and artificial silk industries, and made him not only a great dyestuff chemist but also one of the world's greatest textiles and fibres chemists. His discovery of the effect of weak oxidising agents on woollen fabrics made machine printing of such fibres possible, and also laid the basis for non-shrink woollens. He solved the problem of mildew in dyed textile exports, and made interesting speculations in microbiology, as well as developing methods for decolorising palm oil for the local soap works, and producing iron solutions for medicine. His early work on ferro and ferricyanides, nitroprussides and Prussian Blue was applied not only in dyeing but also in photography, and also formed the basis for his friend Playfair's later researches in pure chemistry.

Playfair, who joined Thomson at Clitheroe in 1841, was an academic chemist trained in Germany. He valued Mercer's friendship, and encouraged him to publish his academic work. In return, Mercer encouraged Playfair to publish, and a relationship of mutual respect developed which led to several major advances in chemistry. Mercer also speculated on the relationship between atomic weights and constitution in chemical compounds and on catalysis. He worked on the nature of bleaching powder and applied this material to deal with a local outbreak of cholera. The other local chemists were good, some very good, but Mercer was great.

PIONEER: WHITTAKER BROS. (ACCRINGTON) LTD.

Walter Haworth

The manufacture of wringing and washing machines at Pioneer Works first began in the year 1886. The three original Whittaker brothers, John, Henry and William, were all members of a large family from Moss End Farm, an isolated and windswept holding 1,000ft. high on the old track between Hapton and Crawshawbooth, below the summit of Hameldon Hill.

Henry must have been of a very adventurous disposition, emigrating to Brazil and establishing a cotton mill at Sao Paulo. This must have been a successful venture, for on his return, it enabled him to put up the bulk of the capital for the continuance of the company, and to build *'Prospect House'* in Whalley Road as his home. Henry died in 1900 and in the following year the firm was formed into a Limited Company, with William as Managing Director at a salary of £182 per annum.

The original entrance to the works was on Arnold Street, the site extending back as far as the railway line; the other premises were gradually taken in, including a slaughter house and a mineral water works. Extensive timber drying sheds with gravity conveyors were built on the higher land, and in 1930 new offices and garages with loading facilities were added on Horne Street.

A variety of distinct departments was required, each with its own foreman, starting with Foundry, Machine Shop, Sawmill, Joiners, Assembly, Painting, and finally Transport. In the early days, steam was the motive power in general use, a Lancashire boiler driving an engine with a huge flywheel, power being transferred through overhead shafting and belt drive to each lathe or machine, being replaced at a later date by individual electric drives.

Demand in the early days was based on *'the bigger the better'*, early mangles being very heavy and cumbersome with rollers up to 24" long and 6" in diameter, the preferred timber being English sycamore or Canadian maple. To satisfy customers' requirements, a large range of models and sizes was called for, which had to be continually improved and updated. During the course of manufacture, when rollers had been turned and bored to take the shaft, cutting to length left thin discs with a central hole, which were in great demand by young boys for use as wheels on home-made trucks.

From the early days, PIONEER had always offered hand-operated washing machines, both large and small, but these, perhaps because of the extra cost, never sold in large numbers, most housewives preferring to do the washing in a dolly-tub with wooden dolly or posser. As models of mangles gradually evolved, they became progressively lighter and smaller, the majority being capable of being folded and fitted with a tabletop, these becoming the bulk of production. Big improvements were made by replacing cast-iron cogs by roller chain drive, followed in turn by machine cut gears, with vitreous enamel in place of the old paint finish, almost always in green and red, a far cry from the old models of previous years. Production at this state of development would be several hundreds wringers per week distributed throughout the country by a fleet of motor waggons. The company had now for many years been under the control of Wm. Whittaker (son of founder) as Managing Director, and of Wm. Haworth (whose mother was one of the Whittaker family) as director in charge of sales, to be followed in due course by their two sons.

Soon after the outbreak of war, domestic production was terminated, and by early 1940 work was concentrated entirely on contracts for the Ministry of Supply. Special purpose machinery was installed and before the cessation of hostilities, outputs included 4 million 20mm Oerlikon tracer shells, almost 3 million fuses for 25 pounder shells, together with hundreds of tons of machine tool casting along with other contracts. Including inspectorate, employees at one time totalled over 300, the bulk being women, some departments working day and night.

For several years after the war, models were generally on similar lines as before, with a substantial increase in sales of domestic step ladders, but then came a big change in demand. A range of small portable wringers with rubber rollers was developed and rapidly became the bulk of production, a large proportion being sold to other manufacturers of small washing machines, but this trade gradually declined. All electric washers were then introduced, but the company had not the financial resources necessary to develop and market these in competition with the highly complex automatics now offered by international organisations such as Hoover and Hotpoint, and was reluctantly compelled, in 1963, to cease production, as were other local firms in the same type of business.

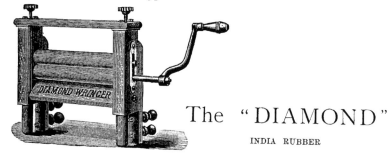

The "DIAMOND"

INDIA RUBBER

CLOTHES WRINGER.

A *'Jinty'* tank engine shunts wagons in the goods yard opposite the Manchester platform at Accrington station in the early 1960s. *(John Searson)*

50

HOWARD & BULLOUGH'S

Jim Wade (Check No. 1474)

The recent demise of Accrington's largest engineering monolith must bring back many memories to hundreds of local people, who, along with myself, spent many years of employment there. *Howard & Bullough's*, a name synonymous with textile machinery throughout the world, made Accrington famous. My own introduction to this rabbit warren of multiple engineering departments commenced in 1934, as a raw, open-eyed lad of 14 years. I started in the spindle and flyer department under the bowler-hatted foremanship of a keen-eyed martinet. When the starting bell went you had to be working within a minute under the watchful gaze of *'bowler-hat'*. There were no canteens, you ate your dinner in the best place you could find; no washing hands before knocking off, no proper guards round machinery. Most machines were belt driven and very dangerous. Everyone, except gaffers, worked in clogs. *'Bullough's'* was a noisy and busy place when in full production.

One of my earliest recollections was to witness the 3 minute concession to the Great War disabled who were allowed additional time to leave the workplace before anyone else, to avoid being knocked down in the rush. Scores of limbless people then worked at Bullough's and made a poignant procession as they made their way home.

I was put through the various initiation ceremonies procedures meted out to all apprentices; sent to the stores for a glass hammer, left-handed screwdrivers, buckets of steam etc. Short time working was the pattern then and Friday afternoon was High Noon time, when the shop clerk came round with the furlough list. Dependent on the amount of work available, this decided how many, and for how long, were laid off. Many fine men, with hard home circumstances, blanched when approached. We suspected that the *'Bosses'* capitalised on this situation by utilising the labour of lads like myself, under 21, from a lower-paid group. If a small order, or orders, came in they would make us do jobs that should have been done by older, trained men, giving us just the minimum of instruction. This period, whilst being hard and taxing to live and work through at the time, served me in good stead later on, for I had to learn a smattering of drilling, milling, tool grinding, emery wheel polishing, oven work etc. The flyers which I worked on came to us initially as misshapen lumps of metal parts, which, after being processed through over 100 different operations, finished as polished, well balanced textile components, despatched to factories all over the world.

Characters abounded of course. Charlie, a labourer who seemed to have dozens of different sets of false teeth and used to grind them to fit on a rough grind stone. Old John, another labourer, deaf and dumb working all day in a world of silence, but somehow able to work miracles by keeping a busy engineering workshop clean and tidy, besides being at the beck and sign of every workman. Old John was always spick and span in his personal clothes and habits, as well as a regular church attender and a model to us all in hard times.

Most machinery was driven by overhead belt transmission powered by a section master motor. If an individual belt broke, the section had to temporarily stop, whilst the repair was carried out. This caused inconvenience to piece-workers in that section, and comments between people were sharp. A number of jobs involved polishing operations on the flyers, where emery wheels and emery bands on fast driven rollers were used. These were dirty jobs and many men took snuff and chewed tobacco to relieve the problem the dust caused them.

Social divisions, even in the workshops, were an accepted thing. This was just a fact of life which everyone seemed to acknowledge. Labourers at the bottom, then hand operators, machinists next, then time served tradesmen, under foremen, foremen managers, and the 'gods' - the directors. One particular director seemed to take it upon himself and took delight in looking after the firm's interests. He always pronounced instant discipline on the spot to anyone who fell out of line. This man probably sacked more men than any other boss or director. When he walked through the works the word soon spread like wild fire. "Joe D.........is on the loose".

I used to enjoy being sent on errands to the other ends of the huge departmental blocks for it meant that I could see for myself what it was to work in the parts of this giant works. To walk through the long, dirty passages that led under the street, to emerge into the vastness of the Moulding Department was like walking into Hades. Big ovens, pouring molten metal into mobile vats, and men pushing the vats along metal rails to different parts of the department where the moulders and their labourers were working on the castings, presented a daunting prospect. The men working with the vats, seeing a raw young lad coming their way, would, in their rough humour, deliberately shake the vat, causing a shower of sparks to fly across my path. Their fun, at my expense, provided a break in their dangerous environment. In spite of their fearsome surroundings, they always seemed to be laughing, joking and singing every time I went through. The next department was the Dressing Shop where the rough castings had their rough edges ground off and then wire-brushed clean. Dust lay thick everywhere and it always seemed to be very cold in there. Things got a bit cleaner in the lower part of the block with the Joiners, Wood Pattern, Tool, Sheet Metal and the huge Planing and Shaping workshops. At the lowest end of Fountain Street were the main offices. Under the main offices, when I started work in 1934, were a series of stables where the heavy haulage horses were kept, and their departure was a distinct change to the modern world.

For a few years after 1934, employment continued unsteadily in starts and stutters, then gradually discussions on the political situation began to appear in the dinnertime conversations, pushing Accrington Stanley, Blackburn Rovers and Burnley from their pedestals. Herr Hitler began to feature more and more. Our labour now seemed to take on a new national importance. The production of armaments gained prominence, brought full employment and also many changes of attitude in the country's workforce. This quickly swept aside the 'old billy-cocked martinet' who swore at people and who sometimes put his foot up your backside if he thought you were too casual with your work. Now we were all in this together and everybody had to give their all. Everyone was all too concerned with one thing only - production. The change from textile machinery making to turning armaments out was achieved in an amazingly short time and new machines were introduced when needed. The scourge of unemployment had now disappeared and it was a case of how many hours could you fit in. The outbreak of war in the late summer of 1939 brought a new sense of urgency and change to everything. The new machines were a welcome change from the old, clapped out, single purpose oddities that had been used repetitively for the same mechanical operation for scores of years. People had to be trained in new skills. Traditional, restrictive trade practices were ignored. If a man showed a willingness and aptitude to tackle a job that had previously only been done by a time-served tradesman he was given the chance to do it, if it meant overcoming a delay in production. Many unskilled and semi-skilled men were given a chance to prove themselves. Substantial

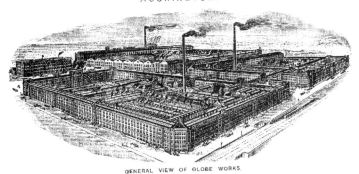

GENERAL VIEW OF GLOBE WORKS.

Founded in 1853. Now occupying, with Extensions, a total floor area of 51·95 acres (210,240 square metres).

numbers of them quickly progressed through the ranks and made fine foremen and administrators.

The new attitudes now permeating through industry brought benefits to all on the social and welfare side. Concerts were held frequently in the works canteen and the workers themselves were given the chance to entertain. The temporarily-defunct Accrington Stanley football ground, Peel Park, was rented for the duration of the war, and after trials, a fine side was formed. This was made up of a number of ex-Stanley players, now working on munitions and a glut of promising amateur discoveries. The first season was spent in playing friendly matches against local works teams and service sides. Crowds of a thousand-plus saw some splendid games. The season after, Howard & Bullough's entered the Lancashire Combination and football was enjoyed at Peel Park until the war ceased. An Amateur Dramatic and Musical Society was formed. Shows were put on at the Hippodrome which played to full and enthusiastic audiences. Under the expert guidance of former Music Hall Variety professionals, Frank and Tom Franks and Norman Entwistle, large numbers of employees were given the chance to display their talent, and many fine discoveries were made.

Of course, all these out of work activities and sports involvements had to fit in with the Number One commitment - the War Effort. Many people were working ten and twelve hours a day, six and seven days a week. Throughout these war years, I felt that I was part of a huge conglomeration of people dedicated to giving all their strength and support to the national cause. People stuck to their individual tasks with a cheerful and steadfast attitude. Armaments were turned out in a constant stream to keep the services equipped with aircraft parts, mine sinkers, shells, etc.

Now my own personal circumstances changed, for I swopped my boiler suit to don uniform and parted from my workmates until demobilisation came in 1946.

Howard & Bullough's was different after the war was over in some ways and yet unchanged in others. The change-over, back to textiles, had been achieved without much upheaval, with much of the new machinery retained and utilised in the new modern approach to engineering. Higher standards and finish were now demanded. Industrial relations were better, as were items like safety regulations etc. Sporting and recreational facilities were first class, especially for cricket and football. The employment position was pretty satisfactory in the first years after hostilities ceased for there was domestic demand for most things. Some people though the management missed their way at this time by not seeing the opportunity to use the plant available by moving the whole or part of it into a different field. Many things were in a bigger demand than were textiles. The motor industry offered opportunities to firms with engineering skills. On the international scene, competition became keen and orders were becoming hard to procure. Changes had to be made all round, and employment began to stutter with reductions throughout the workforce.

The name of *Howard & Bullough's* had long gone and this had taken with it some of the partisan pride of the local people. There were many brave efforts to revive the ailing giant, now called *Platt Saco Lowell*, but we have seen the decline and fall of what was once the heart of Accrington. They say the ghost of old George Bullough still hangs around Fountain Street watching for the men to check in.

ACCRINGTON SWEEPS THE WORLD

In the early 1860s, a group of Accrington businessmen teamed up to manufacture water meters. Their workshop was in Cannon Street, where later was to stand St. James' School. Then, a block of houses, *Ewbank Terrace*, stood there. Their liaison was not successful, and in 1865 the partners split up, leaving James Kenyon and James Entwistle to run the *'Accrington Water Meter Company'*. These two formed a new company - *'Entwistle & Kenyon Limited'*, and decided to move away from meters into knitting machines and domestic hardware, calling their products by the name of *'Ewbank'*. It was to become world-famous and synonymous with the name of the town.

A big advance came to the firm in 1875 when they took on the production of a domestic washing machine invented and patented by another Accrington chap - James Lightfoot Shorrocks. Such a machine had been made in 1873 - *'it was of considerable size and would take four blankets. The wooden rollers on the mangles were 30 inches by 6 inches'*. Shorrocks' invention put the firm on the nation's map.

About 1887, after a fire, the Ewbank Company moved to a 7-acre site off Hyndburn Road. At this time, many variations were introduced to mangles, which were operated by weights and springs.

On 1st May 1889, the company introduced to the world what they claimed to be *'the first practical carpet sweeper made in Europe'*. It swept everything before it. The first was sold to Hiram Waddington, an American joiner. One of the partners had visited America in 1882 to look at business opportunities and had seen a carpet sweeper. The firm's sweepers had names such as *'The Grotesque'*, *'The Collier'* and *'The Griffin'*. The issue of *'The Graphic'* magazine for 26th January 1889 showed a drawing of a missionary giving washing and ironing lessons to natives in Nyasaland, using a Ewbank *'Cottage'* washer, which was available, at extra cost, with a lignum vitae bottom roller. There were five different models, ranging in cost from 4 to 7 guineas.

As the century turned, the company were also making step ladders and vices. In the 1940s they started to make sack trucks and a plough.

In the 1920s, the firm started to spend heavily on advertising. The 1923 *'Ewbank Chronicle'*, a magazine sent to the trade each Christmas, showed five sweeper models:- the

'Success' (£1 14s 3d retail), the 'Conquest' (£2 0s 6d), the 'Magnum' (£2 3s 0d), the 'Empire' (£1 8s 9d) and the 'Royal' (£1 7s 6d). The 'Magnum' and the 'Success' could be had with nickel fitting for about a half-crown extra. At the same time, the mangles ('the mangles with a pedigree') were named 'Victory', 'Treasure', 'Hodder', 'Ribble', 'Trent', 'Little Giant', 'Lady Help' and 'Defiant'. By this time, following the war, rubber rollers and delicate fabrics had arrived. Sober grey had replaced the earlier garish reds, greens and gold of the machines. The company was a leader in trying to please customers. They also lead in staff-management techniques. When the 1930s arrived, porcelain-enamelled finishes were introduced, an attractive, permanent covering for cast iron.

Their 1925 sweeper adverts concentrated on seven selling points:- 7 safety cushions; self-cleaning brushes; ball-bearing brush; armour brush pulleys; unadulterated bristle; solid oak cabinet and a solid-drawn ferrule, which 'gives the assured connection between the sweeper and its handle'. In 1925, a scale-model of a sweeper was presented to the Queen for her famous dolls' house.

All was not plain sailing. A small firm calling itself the 'Tattersall Carpet Sweeper Company' made, in premises adjacent to Ewbank, the 'Boudoir' model. Their 1932 letter-heading declared they were 'established in 1845'. I have doubts about that. Within the town, competitors existed at the 'Pioneer' works, the 'Taywil' (Taylor and Wilson) factory and at Henry Slacks 'Slaxon' works.

In common with many Accrington factories, the wartime years were given over to government work. In 1946, the firm returned to production, and budgeted £6,000 for advertising, which included £500 to be spent in South Africa and £500 in South America.

The 1950s saw the introduction of formica surfaces, and in 1960 the Ewbank Spin Dryer - almost certainly the firm's first electrical product - was introduced at the Hardware Trades Exhibition at Olympia. It cost £29 17s 6d and came in a choice of four colours.

1961 saw the retirement of Maxwell Slater Kenyon, 83 years old, from the family firm, which had been bought the previous year by the Prestige Group for £845,000. 'Mr. Maxwell' recalled August 1924 when they took the whole workforce by train to London overnight, breakfasted on the train then boarded 16 motor coaches for a tour of the capital before visiting the Empire Exhibition, where there was a stand showing 'Ewbank' to the world. He also recalled it being recorded in the board room minutes (1922) that 'it was agreed to resume the practice of paying the cost of soling the shoes of errand boy' (soling and heeling cost 7s 11d, heeling alone cost 2s 0d). Prestige closed down the 221,000 square-feet factory in 1983, and moved production to Burnley. The range of six sweepers then cost between £16.99p and £34.99p. The site was bought by the Asda grocery chain. The spirits of Mr. Entwistle and Mr. Kenyon and their many employees probably do their shopping there.

When the offices were cleared, a framed piece of wisdom was found hanging above the fireplace. Put there by the firm's fathers, who promoted sport among their employees, seeing them as members of the Entwistle and Kenyon families, it read:-

For when the One Great Scorer
Comes to write against your name,
He writes not that you won or lost,
But how you played the game.

A.A.A.: ACCRINGTON'S AUTOMOBILE ASSOCIATION

It is generally accepted that Coventry is the centre of the British motor car industry - but it could have been Accrington.

Automobiles had been in existence but a few years when Alfred Hitchon, a Simonstone-born (1848) blacksmith who, by the turn of the century, had become managing director at Howard & Bullough's, set up a separate company (1904) in premises in Moscow Mill Street, and later Charter Street, called *'The Hitchon Gear and Automobile Company'*. His gear designs were the aspect which made his car better than its rivals.

Alfred had been a prolific inventor since at least 1875 when he registered the first of his 200 patents. In 1901, three of his patents related to automobiles, although he was still working at Bullough's. He was a hard task-master who was reputed to have had the legs sawn off wheelbarrows so that they could not be rested by those wheeling them. Between 1904 and 1907, three Hitchon-Weller models (he had a partner in John Weller of London) rolled off the production lines - it is thought there were about a dozen of each. *'The Globe'* was one of the models - named after the Accrington works.

Hitchon was friendly with Sir Alfred Austin, who gave his name to a famous pedigree of cars, and went with him to the Paris Motor Show in the early years of the century. Their friendship faded when Hitchon discovered his inventions being used in Wolseley motor cars with Austin's knowledge.

The illustration shown, taken from a 1905 magazine advert, is for one of the models, selling at £160.

Hitchon lived in splendour at Clayton-le-Dale. He was exceedingly generous to the new Cottage Hospital. Towards the end of his life (he died in Exmouth, aged 96 years, in 1944) he declined the offer of *'Freeman of the Borough of Accrington'*, an honour he so richly deserved.

Instead of 1950s motorists riding in an 'Austin Cambridge', they could have been behind the wheel of a 'Hitchon Oswaldtwistle'.

This Licence must be carried by the Owner when driving a Motor Car or Motor Cycle and shown to any Police Officer on demand.

No. of Licence 8326   NOT TRANSFERABLE.

COUNTY PALATINE OF LANCASTER.

MOTOR CAR ACT, 1903.

LICENCE TO DRIVE A MOTOR CAR
(INCLUDING A MOTOR CYCLE).

Joseph Taylor

of *497, Manchester Rd., Baxenden, Accrington*

is hereby licensed to drive a **MOTOR CAR**, including a Motor Cycle, for

the period of twelve months from the *Sixteenth* day of

March 1912 until the *fifteenth* day of

March 1913 inclusive.

Received the fee of 5/- for this Licence.

Clerk to the Lancashire County Council.

County Offices, Preston.

Any alteration in Address of Licensee must be notified to the Clerk of the County Council, County Offices, Preston, and this Licence returned for amendment.

4,000/158/10/11.

56

Autocars & Accessories, Ltd.

114, LONG ACRE, LONDON, W.C.

LONDON AND SOUTH OF
ENGLAND AGENTS FOR

The Hitchon-Weller Cars

The
9-h.p.
Hitchon-
Weller
Light
Car

PRICE

£ 160

UNIQUE
VALUE.

The
9-h.p.
Hitchon-
Weller
Light
Car

PRICE

£ 160

ENGLISH-
BUILT
THROUGHOUT.

POINTS FOR CONSIDERATION.

THE ONLY LIGHT CAR on the Market, fitted with the Hitchon Patent Change Speed Gear.

THE ONLY LIGHT CAR with 9-H.P. ınineı Engine with Mechanical Inlet Valve, having variable Lift and Suction Governor.

THE ONLY LIGHT CAR with Automatic Carburettor with Inlet Silencer.

THE ONLY LIGHT CAR with the Hitchon **Three**-Speed Gear and Reverse.

THE ONLY LIGHT CAR having a Live Axle with Worm Drive.

THE ONLY LIGHT CAR fitted with Special Coasting Brake, metal to metal, running in oil.

THE ONLY LIGHT CAR with Pressed Steel Frame, ∩ section.

THE ONLY LIGHT CAR with Patent Safety Friction Clutch adjusted to slip under any strain above the maximum drive of the Engine.

THE ONLY LIGHT CAR which provides a Tyre Box with the same capacity for luggage, tool drawers, battery case, etc., and by which a patented arrangement and construction may be instantly converted into a roomy 4 seated Car.

Having considered these points look round for something of its class to equal it, and you will come back to the " HITCHON-WELLER " at £ 160   , which cannot be beaten.

London and South of England Agents:

AUTOCARS & ACCESSORIES, LTD.
114, LONG ACRE, LONDON, W.C.

ACCRINGTON TOFFEE CANNOT BE LICKED

Wilf Stockley (WS) in conversation with Bob Dobson (BD)

BD *'Stockley's Toffee'* became a phrase synonymous with Accrington. When did your family firm start?

WS My father, Malcolm Vincent, started it when he got demobbed from the Army in 1918. He had made toffee for Tom Hodgson before the war. The Hodgsons were Methodists and so were we. Father sold his toffees on stalls which he rented on markets throughout Lancashire. The toffees were first made in a shed on High Street, Riley's Hill, then for a short time on Paradise Street where he employed staff. From there he moved to a shop in Burnley Road. All the boiling was done behind the shop. This was 1925/6, I was born in 1918. Then came the move to Back Sandy Lane. By this time he had two shops, in Peel Street and in Blackburn Road. Except for the Accrington one, the market stalls had to be closed down in the Depression of the 1930s.

BD What other firms made toffee?

WS *Hodgson's* and *Lightbown's* were much bigger than us. About our size were *Lythe's* (Park Street), *Metcalfe's* (Bold Street) and *Heap's*, who worked in an old brewery in Manor Street. This was in the 1930s. In 1938 there was a British Empire Exhibition held in Glasgow and we exhibited. This was a prosperous time, people had money. After Glasgow, we went to the California Exhibition and I was there for 18 months up to the war. After the war, my father died and my brother Vin and I took over. By now we were in premises in Washington Street, employing 6 to 8 people. In 1947 we moved to Newark Street, increasing our size and turnover, and now wholesaling toffees. In the 1970s, we bought out Tom Hodgson's. They were in Cotton Street. Soon afterwards, we moved into the old Church Kirk School, making mainly chocolate and coltsfoot rock and opening the area's first 'cash and carry' for confectionery.

BD What about the other firms at this time?

WS *Lightbown's* had been bought out by *Cowan's*, a Scottish firm. Their premises were near the *Hargreaves Arms*. Their family concern was noted for coltsfoot rock and *'Grips'*, a throat cough lozenge. After the war, there had been a family split-up and the nephew of the original owner set up on his own. We traded with *Hodgson's* but not with *Lightbown's*. The *Hodgson's* attended Avenue Parade Methodist Chapel with us. They were noted for *'Certs'*, a cough sweet and *'BSM's'*, a caramel made of butter, sugar and milk. Our best known product, and our oldest line, was spanish, honey and butter caramels. When we bought out *Hodgson's*, we discontinued their name but used their premises until the 1980s, when we moved to Blackburn, manufacturing and wholesaling.

BD Did advertising help you?

WS We didn't advertise much, as our market was regional. *Lightbown's* did a lot of advertising. Our Accrington market stall finished about 1960. My brother and I sold the business, with our name, in 1991. I hope it continues for many years.

ACCRINGTON GRIPS THE COUNTRY

Just before the end of the 19th century, J.W.Lightbown started a confectionery wholesale and manufacturing business in Accrington. Amongst his specialities were small black cough tablets, which he called *'Grips'*, probably from the French word which means *'cough'*. During the First World war, the Accrington Pals were asking for them to be sent to France. About 1920, Lightbown's son had taken over the running, and decided to spend £50 on promotion and advertising over a period of six months in the North of England. Business rolled in, and this sum was trebled in the next half-year. Success brought competition as other firms started to copy the product. Lightbown successfully prosecuted a shopkeeper for selling 'Grips' which were *'forgeries'*.

Newspaper editors helped boost sales unwittingly with such headlines as *'Cabinet gets to grips with coalowners'*. By 1928, the firm's 500 customers had grown to 220,073. The many well-designed adverts told that 'Grips' had *'a larger sale than any pastille in the world - they have a "bite" - Stop barking and try Grips'.*

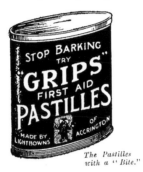

The Pastilles with a "Bite."

GRIPS

First-Aid Pastilles

Will lessen the risks you run when out in cold and damp weather. Put a "Grips" Pastille in your mouth and you will be as warm as toast throughout the coldest, dampest day. "Grips" have a 20 years reputation, and a larger sale than any Pastilles in the world. Avoid all imitations. Insist on "Grips."

10ᵈ·· **CHEMISTS 1/-**

Per Quarter by weight.   Sold by   & CONFECTIONERS Everywhere   Pocket Tins as illustration

MAKERS

Lightbown's of Accrington

EUREKA: THE PHILLIPS BRUSH WORKS

John Phillips Stubbs (JPS) in conversation with Bob Dobson (BD)

BD Before we talk about the Phillips 'Eureka' Brush Works, which I remember as being on Belgarth Road, between Queens Road and the railway line near St. John's School, tell me about a company I've heard of but can find no record of - Tattersall's of 'Boudoir' Works, Accrington.

JPS Tatersall was a copier of the Ewbank sweeper and decided to manufacture a sweeper suitable for small houses in a small section of premises on Hyndburn Road owned by Ewbank at that time. He had a few machines for pressing. He came to my aunt Eleanor, a senior partner in our company, who told him we had a gentlemen's agreement with Ewbank not to make brushes for others. This agreement lasted many years. Ewbank bought this small firm out about 1930 and closed it.

BD When was the Phillips company founded?

JPS In 1863 by Walter Phillips, a time-served brushmaker who came from Pendleton on the new railway. Two years afterwards, the Ewbank company was started. Ever afterwards, the two companies kept to their agreement, were dependent on each other, and prospered. Much later, '*Mr. Maxwell*' (Kenyon) came to us and told us of his expansion plans. He asked if we could borrow £25,000 to buy sufficient bristle to supply them for two to three years. We declined, as we had a policy never to borrow, but he agreed to lend us the cash free of interest, to be paid back weekly as we supplied him with brushes. He was an autocrat whose word was his bond, and whose faith in Phillips was duly repaid. He was succeeded by his son, James, a brilliant engineer.

BD How does the 'Prestige' company fit into your story?

JPS They bought out 'Ewbank (Entwisle & Kenyon) for £1 million in the 1960s. At that time, our production for the firm went up from 10,000 brushes a week to 33,000. During 1963, James sent for me and asked how I would welcome being taken over by Prestige too. We agreed terms and Prestige bought us out in 1966. In the 1970s, Prestige stopped brushmaking in Accrington. They had sold the Belgarth site and had moved the brushmaking section into the Electricity Street part of their building.

BD What should be recorded about the other companies you worked alongside?

JPS 'Pioneer', 'Taywil' and others all nibbled at Ewbank's market but none of them were successful with carpet sweepers. Their biggest competitor for sweepers was 'Short Brothers & Harland' of Belfast, who also used our brushes. Ewbank spent a lot on advertising, and when Prestige took over, they increased it greatly. This helped us buy more machinery. Having a railway in the town was a wonderful aid to business, and another was the fact that Accrington Corporation supplied the cheapest electricity in England.

✷✷✷✷✷✷

After brushmaking ceased in Accrington and transferred to Burnley, the 'Accrington Brush Company' started up in Accrington under Mr. Stubbs' control, eventually expanding into making brushes for electric vacuum cleaners using the redundant Phillips machinery, and later, in Lower Grange Mill, making stretch hoses under a patent held by Mr. Stubbs, who continued with the firm until his retirement in the 1980s.

CUED TO WIN

Jean Webster

'E. J. Rileys, Accrington, where the billiard tables come from' - this was a slogan known all over the world. The enterprise of the firm, with its excellent workmanship, helped to make Accrington known far and wide. It took its name from the founder, E.J.Riley, an amateur sportsman accomplished in the playing of tennis, golf, billiards and other games.

Edward John Riley, born in Accrington in 1856, was one of four sons of a cotton manufacturer and worked for some time in a bank. He eventually left banking and his first venture into the world of sport was the opening of a shop in Abbey Street where he sold athletic goods. (Later E.J.Riley Ltd. retailed general sports goods, having shops at various times in different positions on Blackburn Road.)

Originally a private venture, E.J.Riley's business became a limited company in 1897. When Willow Mills on Dale Street were purchased, about this time, there began a period of prosperity in the manufacture of billiard tables and sports equipment. They were to become the largest makers of billiard tables in the country.

It was in the office in Dale Street where, in the 1940s, I began my working career on the telephone switchboard. I remember being dismayed initially at the tangle of cords criss-crossing in all directions as they were plugged into various extensions. The learning of my job was not made any easier due to a mischievous boy named Robert who, although allocated to *'show me the ropes'*, had only been on the switchboard himself for a matter of weeks!

The main office had a Dickensian appearance, with high, sloping desks to accommodate huge hand-written ledgers. There was wood shelving from floor to ceiling which took care of endless cardboard boxes bulging with miscellaneous papers which jostled for position with lever-arch files. It was while working on the sales ledgers that my knowledge of geography was enhanced because virtually every R.A.F. station and army camp in the United Kingdom was *'on our books'*. Billiard tables were exported (via NAAFI) to the armed forces all over the world.

It was rather an adventure to step out of the office into the factory on the other side of the street. The factory yard was adorned with 'weathering' timber and at some stage, kilns were used for drying it, as before being cut for the making of billiard tables, the timber had to be bone-dry. A lot of time elapsed between the 'weathering' of the timber and the finished article.

The Riley billiard table was synonymous with quality and great skill went into the many stages of manufacture. The slate bed (Italian and $1^3/_4$ inches thick) would be laboriously rubbed for 20 hours so that the error from one end to the other was less than one thousandth of an inch. The mirror-like finish of the polish on the tables was the result of great expertise on the part of the French polishers who worked in a department where an even temperature and clean atmosphere ensured that a very high polish was produced.

Besides the manufacture and repairing of billiard tables, cues were made and re-spliced. Some cues were made to specification; Joe Davis, World Snooker Champion for almost 20 years, lent his name to one of them.

Much skill was used, too, in the re-stringing of tennis racquets and the reblading of cricket bats. Work undertaken in connection with bowling-green bowls included the altering of the bias, the fitting and engraving of new mounts and re-polishing. The bowls would be tested, for absolute accuracy, on a 35 ft. long billiard table, specially built to meet the requirements of the International Bowling Board for whom E.J.Rileys were the official testers.

Nearly all bowls at this time were made either of lignum-vitae (a wood containing little or no sap, and dark brown in colour) or of black 'composition' (a synthetic material). In an attempt to revolutionise the bowling-green bowl, Rileys introduced composition bowls in a range of bright colours - blue, red, yellow and orange (imagine the impact of these colours on the green!). However, this enterprise was not successful because the conservative British bowler preferred the traditional bowl.

Outstanding in the factory was the splendour of the Showroom, with its array of highly polished billiard tables and billiard-dining tables. Alongside them were cues made from English ash and maple with rosewood and ebony butts, similarly polished. The adjacent storeroom was also inviting, with its stock of billiard accessories. There was a great splash of colour with the snooker balls and chalk, together with roll upon roll of billiard cloth, the finest of which came from the west of England.

The most interesting visitor to the Showroom during my time was a well known personality whose arrival caused quite a stir. There was great excitement in the office when someone spotted a luxury limousine, with leopard-skin seats, drawing up outside. We all peered out of the upstairs windows to catch a glimpse of the owner of such opulence in that austere period, and it turned out to be none other than George Formby. He bought a billiard-dining table, but there was disappointment that his wife Beryl did all the talking!

Today, the televising of major snooker tournaments has given further prominence to the game of snooker and the fact that these tournaments are played on Riley tables says much for the prestige of the company established in Accrington a century ago.

THEM LADS FRO' ACCRINGTON

I have come across a poem written, probably in the early days of the Great War, by a writer calling him (her) self 'M.V.P'.

Ah've just bin tryin' to reckon up,
But bless mi if Ah con,
Heaw monny lads fro' Accrington
Hes donned ther karki on.
They've gone fro' every part o' t' teawn,
Fro' t'mansion and fro' t'cot,
At duty's caw they've aw gone forth
To share in t'common lot.
Ah dunno think at matters much
Heaw monny on 'ems gone
We're certain they'll aw do ther best,
Them lads fro' Accrington.

Ther's one or two Ah know reyt weel,
They're med o' just t'reyt stuff.
They're nooan a bit particular,
Let things be smooth or rough.
There's others that Ah carn'd forged
Fer t'sake o' Owd Lang Syne,
When t'rooad Ah throd were aw uphill,
They helped mi monny a time.
An' when Ah kneel mi deawn to pray
Ah think o' every one
An' ax the Lord to bless 'em aw
Them lads fro' Accrington.

There's lots uts gone 'll ne'er come back,
They fill a sowjer's grave,
An' others quite as true an' brave
Lie deep 'neath th'ocean's wave.
An' then there's some ut's sure to come
Wi' a shattered arm ur leg,
Let's trust they'll nooan hev to sit in t'street
Their daily bread to beg.
An' when they land on England's shore
Ah want yo, every one
To give a hearty welcome to
Them lads fro' Accrington.

IN MEMORY OF OUR BAXENDEN LADS
Bill Turner

I stood in a small crowd gathered round Baxenden War Memorial on Remembrance Sunday, 1993. The memorial, a tall granite cross, stands just inside St. John's church yard. Facing the church, an inscription says 'Greater love hath no man than this'. 36 names are inset on the pedestal base. On the reverse are the words 'In memory of our Baxenden lads'.

Just prior to the wreath-laying, three Scouts read out the 36 names - 'Anderson, W., Anderton, J. H., Bailey, H., -and so on. As my eyes followed the names, I realised how impersonal the simple name and initial was. Surely these 'Baxenden Lads', who died in the Great War so long ago, deserve to be better remembered. I decided to find out who these men were and where they lay. The Rev. Mark Ireland gave his support to a plan of action formed over a meal he cooked for us in the vicarage. (Was it Irish stew?)

A visit to Accrington Library brought me to the shelves of volumes of the 'War Graves Commission Registers'. Some 3,500 registers contain almost a million names and my 36 names and burial places were amongst them. A look through the registers of the large memorials in France or Belgium gave me 15 names - a good start. An appeal in the parish magazine brought a lot of information from relatives. As the weeks went by, further library visits brought more details, by checking, inspiration and pure luck.

'Bash Lads' served not just in France and Belgium, but in Egypt, India and Palestine. Lance Corporal Will Hawker lies in South Africa, having died en-route to India from France where he had been wounded. Private Harry Johnson survived many battles on the Western Front but died of 'flu in England and lies with his family not 50 yards from the memorial. Most died in France and Belgium. Some are buried in village churchyards, some in military cemeteries, and others, whose bodies were not found or identified, are commemorated on the huge memorials which are scattered between Ypres and the Somme.

For almost 50 years, the memorial did not show the names of the 'Baxenden Lads' who died in the Second World War. The Rev. Ireland and I decided this should be remedied, so four names were added to the pedestal base. These lads had died in the Indian Ocean, Tunisia, Austria and Scotland.

Research in the pages of the *'Accrington Observer'* enabled me to write a brief biography of the 40 lads. To this I added a brief description of each cemetery or memorial, giving me the basis of a *'Book of Remembrance'*.

My handwriting was transferred into a typed manuscript by Dorothy Tattersall and computerised into book form by Roger Longworth, stalwarts of St. John's. The *'Book of Remembrance'* was bound in fine leather locally and presented to our vicar.

The Rev. Ireland dedicated the *'Book of Remembrance'* at the 1994 Remembrance Day service. In the book, each lad is listed on the day and month order of his death, so that on the nearest Sunday to that date, the vicar will ask the congregation to remember that lad in their prayers. This means that the book is in use throughout the year. It means too that the Scouts can call out the full names of all our *'Baxenden Lads'*. Read them now. Wherever they lie, each lad stands tall. (The final four gave their lives in the Second World War)

William Anderson; John Henry Anderton; Harry Bailey; James Albert Barnes; Thomas Henry Bates; Jack Bolton; Harry Hargreaves Bond; Tom Brandon; Percy Bury; William Thomas Chevin; Walter Dobson; Joseph Downes; Frank Duckworth; John (Jack) Pilkington

Duckworth; Elias Gore; James Greenwood; Benjamin George Hambling; Charles Buckingham Hambling; William Hawker; James Edward Heys; John Lawson Heys; Arnold Hindle; Harry Johnson; Ernest Kenyon; John William Livett; Fred Marsden; James Moss; Fred Ratcliffe; Fred Rushton; John James Skellern; James Edward Smith; Fred Stott; Walter Counsell Todd; David Waterworth; John William Whitehead; Riley Whitehead; Alan Cucknell; Edward Gibson; Wilfred Kavanagh; Richard Winterbottom.

> *'No man in the land stands taller than an Accrington chap thanks to the bravery of these pals'*

NO TIME FER SKRIKING

Alan Bond

In a Lancashire pub hongs a picthur
In a frame on a wa' 'oer a bar
Its geet one mon's name - Tommy Atkins
An' a date, July fost i' t'gret war

'Gis a gill Eli - Tha'rt quiet toneet'
Eli tarned an' stared Tommy i' theen
'Joe Entwistle's mam's geet a telegram'
'Bloody war. T'lad wur ony nineteen.'

'Wod the hell meks em tek yon king's shillin'
An rush to fire t'musket an' t'baw?
Who gis a dam wod'll appen?
Wod the 'ell da they keer? Nod ad aw."

'Id's awreyt fer yon mon o't' pooasters
Tha skens at, pinned up aw ower t'place
Wi t'finger stuck eawt - Country neeads thi!
Aw t'things a blasted disgrace.'

Owd Bert scrawked his pipe eawt i' t'thas oil
An' slowly took yeyd fro' is gill
'Bud fer eawr lads ower theer Tom
Thad anser ta owd Kaiser Bill.'

Tommy thowt ard as he traipsed hoam up t'lone
Heaw wur he beanta tell t'wife
He'd med a decision ta goo an' enlist
Ay, even to lay deawn 'is life.

65

Jem Clegg, barning t'lice fro' his gretcooat
Starred eawt at t'claggy slutch ower t'Somme
'Penny fer t'thowts Jem' axed Walter
'Ah wish ah wer boozin' back hoam.'

'Yon Twaitsis an' Massey's an' Nuttal's best mild
Ay mon, ah con si Eli poo it
T'heyd slarrin' deawn to t'bottom o' t'glass
An' no sign of owd Fritz's bullet.'

'Tommy an' Bert 'll bi lobbin' em back
An' gooin' hooam plaistered o' t'tram
Joe Entie warned bi gooin' na moor
Ah wonder if they infoormed his mam?'

'Tha looks gradley toff i' thi uniform Tom
Ev one wi' me fro' top shelf'
Eli gi Tommy a handshake an' tot
'Good luck Tom, God bless an' good 'elth.'

Sarah Jane wer creym stooanin' er dooer step
Fer Tommy wer soon hooam on leave
He'd penned a few words fro 'sumwheer in France'
Sithi soon bonny lass, darn't ti greeave.

'Fix baynets, stand by, three moor minits'
Tommy stood to 'is ankles i' t'nast
Fire step, ladders, barbed wire an' grass sods
Weer he lay brocken-limbed bi yon blast.

Hoo looked ad his picthur an' grabbed owd o' t'kids
Tears in 'er een geddin' wetter
He'd set off aw wick fro' t'station
An' coom back in a government letter.

Suppin' i silence, snurchin' back tears
Owd Bert supped his gill, nowt wur said
Eli piped up 'Darnd keeap blamin' thisel
Id isn't thy fowt Tommy's dead.'

In a Lancashire pub ongs a memry
In a frame, on a waw ower a bar
Donated bi Tommy's young widder
An' a date, July fost i' t'gret war.

THE 'ACCRINGTON PALS' IN MEMORIAM

George Quinn

To-day is the day, old pal of mine,
I know you remember it well,
When we walked side by side so long ago
O'er the sun-drenched fields of Hell,
Out of the trench, and 'Over the Top',
In the knee high grass to Serre,
We figured old Jerry'd been blown to bits
He'd give little resistance there.

Oh! Christ were we sadly mistaken
And caught in his murd'rous cross fire,
The khaki waves faltered and stumbled
DEATH had reached us in front of the
    wire.
The horrors still remain with me
I can still hear the bursting of shell
The screams of the mortally wounded
And the long rows of dead where they fell.

I recall how we darted for cover
To a shell crater just up ahead.
Past the wounded, the mangled, the
    tortured
Over ground freshly littered with dead.
The thundering guns hurled their anger
And hate, through the concussant air
As safe for the moment we sheltered
In the hole freshly dug for us there.

But then you were hit and I heard you
Collapse, with a low keening cry
And saw the blood-flecked foam on your
    lips.
I knew you were going to die,
I cradled you close in my arms old pal
As a father would comfort his son
I closed your eyes in the last sleep of death
When the life and the spirit were gone.

I lay with you there 'til the night had come
And darkness brought welcome relief
Then returned to the rear with some who'd
    survived
My heart weighted down with its grief
I cursed those who'd used us as pawns in
    their game,
So carelessly wasting our youth
'For King and Country' their battle cry
For THEIR glory and fame was the truth.

The long years have passed, old pal of mine,
And few of us still remain
We're feeble and old and failing fast
But still we remember the slain
Remember the 'Lads of the old Brigade'
The lads who were steadfast and true
And the 'Accrington Pals' of yesterday
Wait to answer the roll call with you.

THE CANARY ISLANDS EXPLOSION
Rev. Philip Schofield

When my father, Walter Schofield, said 'Goodnight' to PC Hardacre they could not have imagined the horror that was to come. They had not met before and PC Hardacre, on patrol at the highly sensitive *'Coteholme'* chemical works in Church, was at first suspicious when he saw my father apparently snooping around.

Dad was a fireman doing a nightly check to ensure that what he called *'pipe-holes'* were clear. In the event of a fire easy access was essential if a major disaster was to be averted, and such a disaster was not unexpected.

'Coteholme', a subsidiary of Blythe's chemical works, employed about 100 people who worked with pictic, nitric and sulphuric acids and manufactured T.N.T.

Herbert Hindle, four years old at the time of the explosion, recalls that workers *'had their faces and hands and hair as well as their clothes turn yellow from contact with the chemical'*. Not surprising that the site became known as *'t'Canary Islands'*! One eye witness said that even dogs roaming the streets turned yellow. By to-day's standards only slip-shod safety precautions were taken. Many wore clogs with metal cokers, a spark from which could easily have ignited the flammable atmosphere, and to safeguard against this they wrapped rags around their clogs.

It was on April 27th, 1917, that the night was shattered by a tremendous explosion. Although PC Hardacre was the only fatal casualty, my father having been the last person to speak to him, a whole community was threatened. It was the bravery of firemen, bringing the fire under control at great risk to themselves, that averted a major disaster. Six of them, three from Church and three from Accrington, were awarded the OBE, my father being one of them.

There are few survivors now alive to tell the tale, and wartime censorship meant that little was reported in newspapers of the time. Under the heading *'Fire and explosion in a Munitions Factory'*, and with a sub-title, *'One killed, Four injured'*, the briefest of reports was given in the 'Accrington Observer'. It stated, *'The Ministry of Munitions made the following announcement yesterday afternoon - The Ministry of Munitions regrets to announce that a fire followed by a small explosion took place at a munitions factory in the North of England early this morning. As far as is known at present, the number of casualties amounts to one killed and four injured'*.

The *'small explosion'* shattered almost every window in Church and, a mile away, the windows of the Co-op Drapery Department in Abbey Street were shattered. The blood red sky, as so many have described it, could be seen four miles away in Great Harwood.

St. James' Church lost all its windows, including stained glass windows designed by Edward Burns-Jones, a pre-Raphaelite artist, and although these were later replaced, others, presented by the Petre family from their private chapel at Dunkenhalgh, were irretrievably lost. They were probably medieval. Herbert Hindle recalls his older brothers, choristers at Church Kirk Church, sweeping up after the explosion and *'providing me with some playthings as we had jars full of the stained glass'*. It was not until August that repairs had been completed and services could be resumed in the church.

Most vividly remembered is the sight of families rushing around in their night clothes, of policemen directing them to higher ground where they might possibly be safer in the event of a further explosion, and the kindness of so many folk who provided the refugees with clothing, food and shelter. My sister, Gladys, recalls being provided with shelter and clothes by a lady in a sweet shop at the bottom of Dill Hall, and how delighted she was with the short pleated skirt in which she could swirl around so that it splayed out.

More macabre is the incident told to Lily Haworth by her mother. There was a lady across the road who had lost a child a couple of days before the bang and she came running out of the house with the little coffin in her arms.

Mrs. Williams, then thirteen and living some miles away in Great Harwood, watched the night sky ablaze with light from her bedroom window which had been rattled by the explosion. She and her brother dressed and rushed to see the fire. They were stopped by the police but not before they had seen windows, doors, and slates shattered and panic-stricken people who were bewildered by it all. Irene Haworth recalls how her mother, a nurse at the Military Hospital at Elmfield Hall, was rushed urgently to the hospital to help deal with any possible casualties.

To my knowledge the cause of the explosion has never been made known, but rumours which were in circulation at the time - of a zeppelin attack or a spy in the works - can be discounted. What is certain is that Superintendent Ware, of the Church Fire Brigade, knowing the serious risk involved, had drawn up a plan of the area and location of the hydrants and open water. It was in accordance with his instructions that my father made his nightly check. It is recorded that the brigade was in attendance within four minutes of the explosion.

My sister recalls that a consignment of T.N.T. was to have been moved on the previous day but for some reason this was not collected. Fortunately it was stored in separate areas of the works, a precaution no doubt taken on Superintendent Ware's advice, and this minimised the extent of the damage.

The Superintendent and five firemen were awarded the OBE, and the citation for my father in the London Gazette of Wednesday, 7th July, 1920, reads, *'For conspicuous courage and devotion to duty on the occasion of a fire at a chemical works'*. No doubt it would be a similar tribute to the other brave men. PC Hardacre was posthumously awarded the King's Police Medal. PC Herbert Bradbury, one of four injured, also received the award. Their bravery undoubtedly limited the blaze and reduced the possibility of a greater loss of life and property.

It was rumoured that PC Hardacre's body was never found. Not true. At great personal risk he closed a magazine door and isolated the fire from more potentially dangerous explosives. Attempting to close a second door, he is believed to have been caught in a blast and thrown against a wall which collapsed and buried him. St. John's Ambulance Brigade in Rishton produced a card with PC Hardacre's photograph on the front, and a poem, *'A Noble Deed'*, written by Kate Leeming. It sold for 2d in aid of the dead policeman's family.

The elder of my two sisters, Winifred, recalled that there had been an earlier scare at *'Coteholme'*. It was on the 27th March and *'in recognition of the excellent service rendered'* the Watch Committee awarded Superintendent Ware £5. The firemen received either £1 5s 0d or £1 1s 0d. There is some confusion in the records as to whether this was payment for attendance at both fires or two separate payments.

It is interesting that the Ministry of Munitions sent a cheque for £47 9s 6d to the Borough Treasurer in payment of charges for attendance at the fire but refused to cover the honorarium paid to the firemen, a total of £29 8s 0d. saying that *'the circumstances do not justify the payment by the Ministry of the grants referred to'!*

Returning home to Canal Street the following day my mother was surprised that a number of curious sightseers were looking through the shattered window of the front room, even more surprised to hear one of the say, *'Just look at them poor kids, they're scared stiff. What kind of parents could 'ave left 'em there?'* My dad was an amateur ventriloquist and *'them poor kids'* were a couple of his talking dolls - thank God there's a place for laughter in even the most frightening of situations!

THE FIRST AND THE LAST - THE ACCRINGTON BOMBS
Peter Smith

The evacuation from Dunkirk was only just completed and France was on the point of surrender when war came to the north west of England. On the night of 19/20 (Thursday) June 1940 single German bombers made scattered raids aimed at ports and industrial establishments from Hampshire to Durham. One penetrated into Lancashire. An air raid alert was sounded for the first time in Manchester lasting from 3.30 to 3.45 am but it was the Accrington district that was to suffer from this first raid of the war.

The raider, on the available evidence, a Heinkel 111 twin engined medium bomber, passed northwards over the town and followed the A680 Whalley road before the local air raid warning siren had sounded. Fortunately the bomber was clear of the dropping zone for the town centre before its first missile fell. It released a succession of thirteen high explosive bombs, two of them of 250 kilos weight, the others of 50 kilos. These were followed by a container of 36 one kilo size incendiary bombs. The container appropriately named an AB36 was designed to spring open during its fall causing its load of incendiaries to reach the ground in a relatively tight group.

The first bomb, a 50 kilo, struck a then unpaved part of Cleveleys Road blowing a small crater eight feet wide and three deep but doing little damage even to some wooden garages in the vicinity. The second fell in the garden of a property belonging to Mrs. Geddie who lived opposite the Crown Inn on Whalley Road. It blew a crater 12 feet wide and damaged a coal house. Two other properties on Whalley Road suffered. A big bungalow named *'Netherby'* took a direct hit from a 50 kilo bomb and was shattered, later to be rebuilt. The occupants, Mr. George Belsey and his sister Miss Hetty Belsey were lucky to escape serious injury. Mr, Belsey was a former East Lancashire scout commissioner. The other property *'Hasledene'* the home of Mr. G.C.M.Barlow took a 50 kilo bomb on its front lawn. It blew a crater 12 feet across and five deep, knocking over the front wall and railings for some sixty feet. It cracked a gas main and damaged the pavement. Although the house was only 25 feet away from the crater and its ceilings were cracked there were luckily no serious injuries. Remarkably no windows were broken in surrounding property. In contrast the next bomb was fatal. Mrs. Mary Ramsbottom aged 65 and her daughter Beatrice aged 21 were both killed when Fielding Terrace facing on to Whalley Road and backing on to Walton Street was struck by a 50 kilo bomb. The father Mr. Ephraim Ramsbottom aged 66 was taken to hospital seriously injured and he died there next day. The son, also named Ephraim, aged 28, who had been sleeping in the back bedroom was uninjured and escaped through the bedroom window. A neighbour, Dennis Butler, needed stitches to a head wound and his wife was badly shocked. The neighbours on the other side of the Ramsbottoms, Mr.

The *Manchester Guardian* showed this picture on 21st June 1940, but identified it only as *'...in a North-Western town where two people were killed during the raid yesterday morning.'* The houses, 41 and 43 Fielding Terrace, Whalley Road, have not been replaced.

and Mrs. Fred Newsham and their son Alan fortunately escaped injury. The bomb which struck the front of the Ramsbottom's house, No. 43, penetrated right through the structure and exploded in the soil underneath. There was little blast damage to surrounding property except Nos 41 and 45 adjoining.

The aircraft then passed over the vicinity of Enfield brick works and the western fringe of Whinney Hill, where its bombs fell to little effect. One in a clay pit made a shallow crater 9 feet across. Another must have penetrated more deeply for it left a clean entry hole 12 inches wide which was later examined by a military bomb disposal team who decided that the bomb must have exploded leaving a camouflet, an underground cavity, without cratering the surface. The next left a crater twelve feet across and four deep near a stone wall which remained undamaged. A turnip field took one which blew a 15 feet diameter crater four feet deep in clay and sandstone rubble.

The next to fall was one of the 250 size high explosive bombs. This hit an unpaved track of ashes and rubble. It blew an oval crater 24 feet by 12 feet, 6 feet deep, throwing debris on to a matchboard chicken house breaking a couple of windows and no doubt ruffling a few feathers. A 50 kilo missile in a turnip field then made a crater 15 feet across by 5 deep. A larger crater 24 feet across and 10 deep was made by the next 250 kilo bomb which fell in a grass field having six inches of soil over sandstone. This was scattered up to 200 feet. Two 50 kilo bombs fell in the same field 120 feet and 200 feet from the larger one.

Banking to its left the bomber again approached Whalley Road, this time at its junction with Sparth Road. It was here that the incendiary canister was released showering its 36 separate missiles.

In the second bungalow in Whalley Road below the Sparth Road junction Mr. Joe Wiggins was in bed with his wife when one incendiary fell through the roof on to the bed and broke his leg. He was taken for treatment to the civil defence first aid post which was in the basement of the old Clayton-le-Moors Town Hall and afterwards to hospital. All the incendiary bombs were concentrated within a quarter mile square. Several fell in the garden of *'Sparth House'* on the north side of the junction, one of them in a children's sand pit. The fire brigade dealt with one that lodged on the roof of the house. The house on the opposite corner was also damaged. Councillor J.R.Houldsworth lost most of his clothes at his house on Whalley Road when his wardrobe was burned out. At 10 Dryden Street, occupied by Mr. Bolton, an incendiary lodged in the bedroom ceiling from where he dislodged it and it fell blazing on to the floor where he was able to extinguish it with heaped sand and soil from the garden. A house next door to the shop at the corner of Milton Street and Whalley Road, occupied by Mrs. Middleton was badly burned. Other incendiaries burned themselves out in the streets and roadway.

On the early morning of 24 December 1944 Hitler made his most ambitious use of air launching in a single attack aimed at Manchester, Forty five V-1s were launched from a position some 40 miles off the east coast opposite Hull and thirty one of them crossed the coast. Half of these fell within a twenty mile radius of Manchester. Lancashire received eight of the missiles.

'Lower Westall Farm' stands to the left of the A677 Haslingden-to-Blackburn road within the boundary of Oswaldtwistle but only two and a half miles from Accrington town centre. As the road takes a turn to the right, the track leading to the farm goes up an incline to the left. To the right of the track and short of the farm is the sloping meadow in which a V-1 exploded at 6 am. This was the last of the Lancashire flying bombs and the last enemy weapon ever to fall in the county. Local people had plenty of warning on this occasion as the air raid alert was sounded at 5.28 am. The crater blown in the meadow was 12 feet across and 5 deep. Roof, door and window damage was done to the farm and nine other farms and cottages. A small pottery works also suffered damage but luckily there were no casualties resulting from this incident. Extensive blast damage was a feature of the V-1 which had an 1870 lbs (850 Kg) warhead of the most powerful explosive.

Four and a half months later came VE Day. Accrington had seen the first and the last of the air raids.

✱✱✱✱✱✱

For a full account of the V-1 attack upon the region, see Peter Smith's book *'Flying Bombs over the Pennines'*.

MY EARLY SCHOOLDAYS IN ACCRINGTON

Dennis Duckworth

Like my mother and father before me I was sent at the age of five to the Swedenborgian day-school in Hargreaves Street. My parents and grandparents had been children there when the school was in its heyday, but I was there at its demise. It was a church-founded, church-sponsored, *'free'* school for popular education, a product of early nineteenth century enlightenment and philanthropy, inspired by the wish to instil standards of spiritual truth and good behaviour in the minds of the young. The governors and most of the teachers were members of the New Church. But by the end of the first World War it ceased to exist as an educational institution. Increasingly the teaching of children was becoming the responsibility of the town and the state, and the problems of the upkeep of old buildings, amenities, equipment, and salaries were growing more difficult for private educationalists. So in 1918 the old familiar classrooms were transformed into a Young Men's War Memorial Institute, with billiard-tables and dartboards, and we little children were dismissed to go to other schools. Similar catastrophes were happening throughout the entire land, and old-style nonconformist education was being pressed out of existence. Was it a mistake? Looking back, I think it was unfortunate, but can the inevitable ever be called a mistake?

My teacher in the infant class at Hargreaves Street was Aunt Polly, but this did not make life any easier for me. She was not one to countenance any family favouritism. A compelling and unforgettable teacher, she stood before us high-collared, long-sleeved, leather-belted, and long-skirted - and talked to us as we sat wide-eyed, open-mouthed and spellbound. She made great use of her attractive, melodious voice, and also of what she called her *'signal'* - a piece of turned wood against which a wooden peg was fastened with twisted string, so that with a flick of the thumb a sharp clicking sound was made: the signal. It was the age of obedience. The first rule of the school was, to obey. We stood up, sat down, marched, stood still, stopped talking, etc., etc., all to the *'click'* of the signal. With our slate-pencils and slates we drew the curves and *'pot-hooks'* which were the basic shapes of writing. And we learned to read in the alphabetic way, long before psychology brought in the *'look and learn'* method of reading. I can remember quite clearly the whole class of little children standing in a wide circle, each one with an alphabet card containing a capital letter suspended from his neck. If he could recognize and say his letter, well and good, but if not, he was hit on the head with the card! It was good fun - basic education at its simplest. I also remember a rocking-horse in the corner of the room, a doll's house, and some building-bricks.

When the school finally closed, and I was seven, I was accepted at the nearby Benjamin Hargreaves (St. Paul's) Junior School. This little stone-built school at the edge of the town stood on gently sloping land, giving a playground on two levels. It was bathed (in my memory) in perpetual sunshine. We sat in class and could hear the bleating of sheep, the braying of a donkey, and the crowing of a cock. The classrooms were just partitions, and the teachers and children alike needed to raise their voices in competition with their neighbours. The cloakroom had a double row of iron hooks and a single diminutive sink. The outside lavatory was repellent even to young boys - an open drain, two or three doorless cubicles housing high seats over deep holes, and flushless. Yet eternal spring seemed to surround the school and the vigour and warmth of young life mellowed its imperfections.

The interior of New Jerusalem School, built in 1836, demolished in 1886. The chairs and forms are set out for Sunday School. The gas lights have no mantles - just a jet.

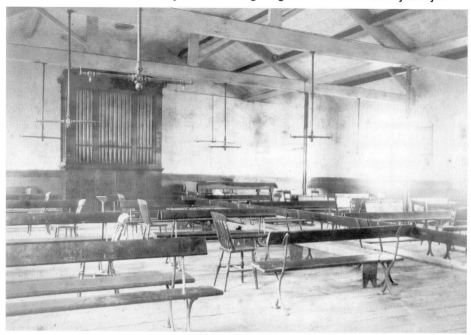

The headmistress - *'Little Bell'* - was a virago who used the school as a whipping post. Though only slight she could be intensely fierce, and there was not a boy and hardly a girl at Benjamin Hargreaves who did not taste her cane. The teaching staff comprised four elderly ladies and one young apprentice. Mrs. Bale possessed a certain motherly roundness, Miss Spike was bespectacled and thoroughgoing, Miss Mastairs was a stiff and ritualistic priestess, while Miss Hearty of the reception class - in spite of her name - was gentle and self-effacing. Annie Pendleton, the apprentice, was about eighteen, and the others could have been no more than thirty-five - far too old to teach, we thought! Little Bell would be barely forty. They were all devoted to their calling and therefore wonderfully successful teachers. I remember them as slow in their movements, harsh of voice, somewhat haughty in demeanour, moving amongst the children as in a restrained ballet.

I have no recollection of being taught by Little Bell herself, though her cane left an impression on my mind more lasting than the white and red weals on my hands and legs. My most vivid picture of her is an extraordinary one. She did something quite astonishing before all of us: in November, soon after my arrival, she summoned the whole school together and then stood on a table in front of us. She said, *"The war is over at last. Peace has been declared. The soldiers will come home, perhaps your own fathers and older brothers. It is the armistice".* Tears moistened her sallow cheeks. We sang a hymn and *"Keep the home-fires burning".* She pointed through a window to the hill overlooking the town,. *"There, can you see the wood being piled up for the bonfire? It will be lit tonight, and you must go out and see it blazing so that you will always remember".* We looked at her with innocent eyes as she was helped down from the table. Mother told me at home that

74

Little Bell's only brother had been killed at Gallipoli. That night we saw the beacon ablaze on the Coppice.

In my four-and-a-half years at the little church school I know that I imbibed much mental and spiritual sustenance. I have never forgotten what I learned there, and much of what I have discovered in life has seemed to be a further growth from the soil of my early schooling. Why were those years so important? Was it the system, the excellence of the teaching, or the receptivity of the child mind? Probably all of these. The curriculum was ordinary and typical. We were drilled to memorise much from the four books of Palgrave's Golden Treasury. I remember the wooden boxes with leather straps which were opened on the classroom floor, housing Hawthorne's Wonder Book and Tanglewood Tales, copies with good black type on thick yellow paper and with Arthur Rackham's superb illustrations. I loved the little naked Pandora and even admired the writhing snakes in Medusa's hair. Music was encouraged. We sang Handel and Purcell and many a good English ballad: *'The Lass of Richmond Hill'*, *'The Bailiff's Daughter of Islington'* - and also much tonic-sol-fa. The tonic-sol-fa classes stand out in my mind as perfectly representative of the education of the 1920s: the chart hanging on the blackboard, the teacher's cane darting among the soh-la-te's, and the ladder of our scales rising up to the rafters.

Some children in my class were sparsely clad and poorly shod. My schoolboy friends wore short trousers topped by a woollen jersey or jacket, often in holes. Long trousers were never seen on little boys. Girls wore a knee-length frock or smock over a slip, and sometimes a pinafore. Boys and girls alike wore clogs, but there were some who did not have stockings or socks. Nor did all small schoolgirls wear knickers or drawers, as our rough-and-tumble games clearly showed. *'Hygiene'* was a new word - a favourite word on the teachers' lips, and the tang of Condy's Fluid (potassium permanganate) pervaded the classrooms. Ringworm was common, as were sore eyes and scabs. I do not think that one child completely escaped having nits in the hair, and in those pre-vitamin days there was plenty of evidence of malnutrition - bow-legs and knock-knees. The appearance of *'spots'* was a cause of alarm and rightly so, for an outbreak of serious infection was a much greater possibility then than now. In my few years at Benjamin Hargreaves I can remember one smallpox case, three of scarlet fever, and a diphtheria epidemic in which some children died. We also held the belief - which I later discovered to be a common persuasion of the Pennine towns - that too much fresh air indoors was chilly, draughty, and unhealthily dangerous. There was also some evidence at school of rough treatment at home: the two small Kane sisters sometimes came in the mornings bearing the bruises and scars from their drunken father's belt. Yet in the main we flourished. I think of my schoolmates then as bonny, rosy-cheeked, full of energy and fun. The boisterousness and rude vigour of our childhood was a part of our semi-countrified life.

There was little to disturb the inconsequentiality of my school-days except the appearance of the blue and pink cards on the teacher's table once or twice a year foreboding a visit by the doctor and a medical examination. Nothing daunted me as much as those cards containing the particulars of my name, address, age, sex, height, weight, number of teeth, and whether I had had measles, whooping-cough, chicken-pox, or anything else. When I saw those cards deposited there next to the ink-bottle and chalk-box I was plunged into instant misery

The Medical Officer of Health came in person to examine us - Dr. Richard Greyloop, fierce, eccentric, and downright, but a very dependable medical man. He was well known

75

in the town. He wore a bowler hat over a Kaiser moustache, had clogs on his bare feet, and rode a horse - which he tethered to the school gate. *"Show me your tongue - good! Chest - breathe in. Any spots? Where - let me see? What do you like to eat?" "Jelly"* I answered promptly. *"So do I"* said Dr. Greyloop. *"What else?" "Nothing else, only jelly,"* I said. *"Put him down for the Craven Heifer,"* he said to the nurse, passing on to the next child. The Craven Heifer was a newly-opened Ribble Valley children's convalescent and holiday home. My parents were interviewed and gave their consent. I went there for three weeks, and it is strange that I have no memory of that lovely old house standing by the river and surrounded by meadows and thickly-wooded hills, but only of the taste of the creamy milk on our breakfast porridge and of mother's Sunday afternoon visits by charabanc when she wore a hat from which a long pheasant's tail drooped gracefully over her shoulder.

I left Benjamin Hargreaves Primary School just before I was eleven to go - to Little Bell's amazement and apparent chagrin - first to the newly opened Central School and later to the Grammar School. I did not leave unequipped: I had the Three-Rs, some poetry, classics, art, music, and what I grew to value increasingly in future years, history taught in terms of the life we saw around us - Miss Spike's speciality and passion. Of all the schools in my life - and there have been many - I feel that I have become what I now am because of the wisdom, discipline, and positive zest which I encountered in those five years at Benjamin Hargreaves.

Technical School & Arcade, Accrington

This 1910 postcard shows the Grammar School in Blackburn Road. In the background, the purpose-built shops still have their covered arcade frontage.

THE GRAMMAR SCHOOL

The Corporation's Education Department built a new Technical School on a Blackburn Road site and its first pupils enrolled in 1895. In 1921, the emphasis on teaching there shifted from a technical syllabus to one concentrating more on academic subjects, though throughout the years up to 1975, when government policy dictated that 'elitist' schools should be replaced by 'comprehensives', some time was given over to subjects such as woodwork. The school was never ideally-situated, as its sports fields were a mile away at the top of Willow Lane. I don't wish to go into the whole history of the school, but I do want to draw attention to the number of pupils who, acorn like, became oak trees in society. Elsewhere, I mention some who achieved eminence. Sadly, there are no records available of any - and there would be some - who guested in H.M.'s detention rooms.

I do want to quote from the pens of two of the school's masters - Headmaster 'Ben' Johnson and Deputy Head Lou 'Pug' Portno. They felt the school's pulse and gave out the medicine. They wrote in the school's final magazine:-

Mr. Bernard. Johnson, Headmaster, 1941-1967.

My colleagues and I strove, in completely inadequate premises and at a time of great difficulty, to maintain high standards of scholarship, conduct and responsibility, and the greater problems we faced, the more we loved the School.

When a distinguished person dies he is commemorated by a service of thanksgiving for his life and work. In the same way, I feel that we should express our pride and joy in the achievements and influence of Accrington Grammar School. The late Sir Percy Lord once described it as a great school, and I believe he was right. For eighty years it produced hundreds of pupils of the highest intellect and character, whose parents unstintingly supported the School and made untold sacrifices for the good of their sons and daughters. It was splendidly staffed by scores of able and dedicated men and women, and it was governed in an enlightened and liberal way by people who were proud of the School and anxious for its welfare. In consequence, the reputation of the School spread far beyond the confines of its county and even of its continent. I still hear from former pupils in distant parts of the world, men who acknowledge what they owe to the training and inspiration they received at School.

Administrative changes in education can only be justified if they result in wider opportunities for all the boys and girls in the schools and a raising of the intellectual and moral standards of the whole population. If they do not have this effect, then the destruction of schools like Accrington Grammar School is an unpardonable crime. Only time and experience will show whether education in this country has benefited or not.

Louis Portno, 1927-1967.

Never let it be said that the Grammar School was interested exclusively in the academically able. No boy at school was ever condemned, nor should be, because of a lack of ability, and this has always been the policy of successive Headmasters and staff. A boy was never censured for inability, but only for unwillingness. It has always been recognised in the School that some boys can never do well in certain subjects nor, occasionally, in all of them. But as long as they give of their best and make every effort then they are given every encouragement and praise, and more often than not such boys will start to improve.

Furthermore, never, never let it be said that the Grammar School educates only the sons of the middle-classes, whatever the term may mean today. From my own knowledge of the home circumstances of many of my old pupils this is patently untrue. Moreover, some years ago, long before the era of wage-packets of £60 to £100 per week, I had occasion to consult the School entry registers in order to discover the addresses of some old boys. Amongst the relevant information about each boy was an entry giving the occupation of the father. In the majority of cases these entries read monotonously - *'labourer, labourer, labourer, cotton operative, caretaker, labourer, etc., etc.'*

THE END OF TERM

In June 1876, young Emily McKenzie, a pupil at F.N.Haywood's Peel Park Academy, wrote a letter from her classroom to:-

My dear Parents,

One of the most pleasing duties at school is to write announcing the coming of holidays. This I have much pleasure in doing at this time.

The present session will terminate on Friday 16th instant and the school will re-assemble on Monday July 24th.

By an examination of the contents of this and my other school books, you will ascertain the kind of work I have done in the half year, as well as the way in which I have conducted myself at school.

I hope you may be on the whole satisfied with me, and that your care for my welfare may be repaid in some measure by a future career of uprightness and useful activity on my part.

Believe me, Your truly affectionate daughter.

Note that the private school got six weeks holiday.

MOSELEY'S BREAD

One of my childhood memories is of being in a gang of lads and lasses, on a day during the school holidays, going exploring in Woodnook. We found ourselves in Grange Lane at the corner of Jacob Street outside Moseley's Bakery - they called it 'Borough Bakery'. (I recall thinking that their bread was tasteless compared with the real bread my grandma baked or that we bought at bakers' shops, but I did like the fact that it was already sliced thinly, and, by the late 1940s, wrapped in greaseproof paper. This had a horse's head on, and the clever words 'Thoro'bre(a)d')

Our efforts at scrounging or pinching something to eat came to nowt, so we sang out, loudly so as to attract and annoy the bakery workers before running away in case they came out, captured us and took us to the nearby 'cop shop'. The delightful song went:-

> Oh, don't eat Moseley's bread
> It makes you shit like lead,
> No bloody wonder you fart like thunder
> - Don't eat Moseley's bread.

FROM LILIAN'S LIPS

In 1972, Mrs. Lilian Pratt of Plantation Street, wrote down her memories for her grand-daughter. Her parents were William and Mary Bew, who kept a grocery and medicines shop in Wellington Street, near Timber Street and Grange Lane. She started by recalling her very early days. She was born in 1906.

I have been trying to think of some of the first things I can remember of those days. I must have only been 2 years old when the old steam trams finished running and the electric trams came into being. I have vivid recollections of standing in Manchester Road and watching them puffing up the steep incline towards Baxenden. There was a firebox underneath at the front end and red hot cinders would sometimes fall out on to the road. There were times too when the passengers would get out and walk a short distance then re-enter when the steam was well up. I also remember many accidents at the corner of Grange Lane by the shop. If the brakes on horse-drawn lorries were faulty the horse could not always keep the heavy load behind them in control and they would come crashing down the road and the horse would be killed. One very bad accident occurred like that and the horse ran into a postbox - a round one - standing on the pavement. The horse and driver were killed. The box was smashed by the shafts of the cart and the letters inside were brought into our house to be washed free of blood and returned to the General Post Office. After that, the box was placed in the wall.

Another early recollection is of a man with a huge brown bear which danced around a pole. He usually came about dinner-time to the top of the lane and Grandpa or Father would take a loaf out for the bear to eat. He came every year around Easter until the 1914-18 war started. The organ grinder and his monkey were often seen around. The monkey wore a little red cap with a black tassel on top. He used to sit on top of the organ for a while then jump down and dance on the ground. He would then take off his cap and go around to the onlookers asking for pennies. I watched all this from the house window.

Church and Sunday School played a great part in our lives. Remember there was no radio or TV in those days and all our entertainment took place in our Sunday Schools. There were wonderful concerts, 'At Homes', Lectures, Tea Parties, Magic Lantern Shows, Bazaars, and Field Days in the summer. I was very fortunate to always attend a fully-graded school. Even back in 1908 we had separate departments for Beginners, Primary, Junior, Intermediate and Senior scholars. There was too a Men's and Ladies' Class, all well attended. We had very devoted leaders and teachers. School began at 9.15 am then we went to Church at 10.30 am till noon (no short 15 minute sermons in those days!). Home to dinner and back to school at 1.30 pm until 3.00 pm. At night there was a Children's Service as well as the adult service but I never went to that Children's Service - I had to go to bed soon. Sunday was a very special day and preparation for it began on Saturday night when I remember mother getting Grandpa's tall black hat out of its box and carefully wiping it round with a green velvet pad, then laying it on the table in the front room along with his stiff starched cuffs and rolled-up umbrella. He always wore a black tail coat on Sundays and looked very smart. Father's clothes were also brought out of the wardrobe but he wore a black bowler hat and ordinary suit. Grandma Bew was very deaf and she did not go to church often. Her dress consisted of long black skirts to her feet. A bonnet with perhaps gay flowers tucked in, or sometimes feathers and a sealskin coat and black kid or lace gloves. On Sunday afternoons she used to sit in her rocking chair and sing hymns she had learned as a little girl in the Higham Sunday School. I still remember the words of those hymns!

When I got home from school with my parents and Auntie Mary I was allowed to look at the pictures in the big Family Bible or sometimes my mother read to me. I always asked for a book called 'Hope On', the story of an orphan girl who stole a loaf of bread from a baker's van for her starving brothers and sisters. She got caught but I have forgotten what happened afterwards. I remember the story always made me cry but I always asked for it. Father used to smoke his ONE cigar of the week. I never saw him smoke on any other day and never a pipe or cigarette. It was a nice cosy time, all nice and snug in that front room. We had a piano in the room too. Auntie Mary was learning to play and then I started to learn later. Grandpa Bew was Secretary of a Bible Class at 'Wesley'. This was where the very, very old ladies and gentlemen went. They were too old for the men's or ladies' class. I remember the ladies all wore bonnets so they must have been old. Very often the preacher at the morning service would stay and take the class in the afternoon and this meant that we very often had to have him to dinner at our house. My! I had to be a very good girl that day! After dinner he was put in the front room, to have a little nap I suppose or to look over his lesson.

I was 3 years old when I started day school - the very day Woodnook Council School opened in 1909. It was a lovely modern building, so light and airy, quite different to the old day schools in the town. We had lovely toys to play with and a grand rocking horse and a big hammock in the Baby Class. Miss Hargreaves was my first teacher and Miss Swift the headmistress.

All the boys and girls in those days wore clogs and they did keep our feet nice and warm. Shoes and boots were only for Saturday and Sunday wear. When I was six years old my little brother was born and he was given the name William. He was a strong happy little boy and I was glad to have someone in the house to play with. We had lots of good times together. Holidays with our parents were usually taken on the West Coast, Morecambe or Blackpool. Very few people went to the East or South Coasts and if anyone went across to the Isle of Man we thought they were very rich! When we went on picnics, there were no buses to take us to Whalley, only the tram to the canal bridge at Clayton and then we had to walk. In 1914 the Great War broke out - I was 9 - and very interested in maps where our soldiers were fighting in France. There was no radio or TV and people went to the Newspaper Office in Dutton Street to SEE the news posted in the window. Very early on we had Belgian refugees sent to us and they were housed in a large house opposite the Hospital in Whalley Road. We had a very large munitions factory in the town and women went to work there as more and more men joined the forces. Food was rationed and we saw the end of white flour. The bread made from horrible grey-brown flour was awful to eat. Families where the father had joined the army or navy were very poor and could not always pay for food. Grandpa Bew always saw that none of his customers with children went short of the essential food and although several families owed him a lot of money, there were only three families who did not pay back all they owed when the father came back from the war. My father was considered too old to join the army but he had to do other war work and he went up to the Hollins Farm owned by the Newhouse family and taught them how to plough and sow wheat etc. All farmers were compelled to put their land to the growing of foodstuffs. Small allotments became the order of the day and people grew potatoes etc. in their front gardens and kept a hen or two in their back-yards. Sugar was in very short supply and jam just disappeared as did sweets and chocolates. Many things were rationed. Everybody was knitting socks, scarves, helmets and mittens for the soldiers. At day-school we sent dozens of pairs of mittens to one of our ships and had letters back from the sailors. Wounded soldiers came to Calderstones Hospital and some came to our Isolation Hospital which was used as a Military Hospital. Every week we had a collection at Day-school and food was sent up there. One week everyone had to bring a potato - the next week an onion - then a carrot - a piece of soap - one egg. It was surprising how much it amounted to from all the scholars. In return they sent us two passes which were given to children in standard 5 or 6 and we were allowed to visit on Sunday afternoons. We also had Flag Days in the town and I sold flags - today I think you have to be 16 before you are allowed. Accrington suffered greatly when in one battle almost the whole of our Accrington Pals Battalion was wiped out in France. There was hardly a street in the town where someone had not lost a father or relative that day. Our family in one sense was spared - we only had one cousin of my mother's killed, and he was in the Seaforth Highlanders. Lots of young men from our church were killed and when the others returned in 1918 we missed them very much.

In 1914 my other little brother was born but he only lived seven weeks. In 1916 another blow came when my 5 year old brother, William, died of meningitis; no cure was known in those days. This came as a great shock for, unlike me, he had always been a very strong healthy boy. I was the one to have measles, chickenpox and whooping cough. Now I became a very lonely little girl and the house seemed very strange indeed - no one to romp around with - no one to tease. I was learning to play the piano at the time and I used to escape into the front room whenever people came to the house because I did not like to hear them talking to my mother about William. I certainly knew my piano pieces during those days. I felt too that my mother was not at all interested in me - not that there was any lack of love from anyone in the house, but losing two little boys must have been dreadful for her, and father too.

Well, the war ended and so to did my school days - I forgot to tell you that at our Cookery Lessons all my recipes were, of course, meatless and they came in very useful during the Second World War when meat was rationed again.

81

CHILDHOOD IN ACCRINGTON (1950s)

Antony Portno

Until I was eighteen, in 1956, I lived with my parents in Hollins Lane, Accrington, just above the upper entrance to Oak Hill Park; My grandparents, William and Edith Haworth lived next door, at Holly Mount. When I was five, I started attending Woodnook School but after two years or so, it was converted into a Secondary Modern School and no longer accepted children of my age. The alternative schools available were Spring Hill and Peel Park.

I was sent to Spring Hill and well remember walking there each day. The route took me along Nuttall Street and under the railway bridge turning right at the end by Highams Mill into Victoria Street. Along this street were a number of small engineering workshops. Men in overalls stood outside on the pavement smoking Woodbines and Full Strength Capstan. Small trolleys contained piles of bright metal coils, the by-product of turning steel, copper or brass. They were covered in oil and gleamed. They seemed attractive but they were brittle and very sharp.

To get to Spring Hill from Victoria Street I had to make my way across a grid of streets, mostly paved with large, sandstone cobbles, in order to maintain a diagonal direction up the hill. I used to vary my route from day to day and would sometimes climb up Carter Street, a street so steep that a row of posts across the top barred it from use by traffic.

As I made my way to school, I saw plump ladies in floral smocks embellishing their doorsteps by rubbing them with donkey stones, a soft chalky stone in yellow or white which coloured either the entire step or, sometimes, just the edges. The housewives would often place crystals of washing soda on the coping stones of the low walls around their front gardens. When it rained, the crystals dissolved, cleaning the stone and destroying any growth of moss.

Spaced along the coping stones was a series of small pits filled with lead, in which were embedded square stubs of iron. These were the remains of railings which had been cut off as a source of iron for munitions manufacture during the war. The front doors of many of the houses were painted in facsimile of wood grain, every knot and curl in the grain of the wood painstakingly combed into the wet paint by a skilled decorator.

The Headmaster at Spring Hill was William Spencer. I remember him as a fierce man who moved from one place to another in a series of short dashes. He caned me several times for crimes I no longer recall. The school had a fine record of eleven-plus passes and much of the work was directed at coaching pupils in the skills of answering large numbers of short questions at high speed. Accuracy was not a primary consideration. Forty correct out of fifty attempted, scored more highly than thirty-five out of thirty-five. I sat next to a boy who was clever, careful and accurate but slow. He failed his eleven-plus. I remember thinking this was unfair. I still think so.

Mr. Spencer would, from time to time, burst into the classroom unannounced in the middle of a lesson. Ignoring the teacher, Miss Hindle, he would select at random a hapless child and, pointing an interrogatory finger, would bellow *"Twelve twelves"*. Sometimes he might vary the routine with an alternative problem from the higher reaches of the multiplication tables. The correct answer, I remember, was not *"one hundred and forty-four"*. It was, *"one hundred and forty four, sir"*. Omission of the '*sir*' was as grave an error as answering *"one hundred and twenty-three"*.

At the age of eleven I transferred to Accrington Grammar School, where my father taught French and was Deputy Head. I used to walk all the way there too, down Royds Street, across to Wellington Street, round by the swimming baths, under the railway bridge and along by Howard & Bullough's until I reached Willows Lane and turned right by E. J. Riley's into Blackburn Road just short of the school. Sometimes I indulged myself and caught the bus home. This entailed walking along Blackburn Road to the Town Hall. From there a red and navy blue Accrington bus, a pale blue and cream Haslingden bus or a maroon and cream Rawtenstall bus, would take me to Bamford Street for a penny. I would then walk up through the rockery in Oak Hill Park and, opposite the bowling green, take an illegal short-cut through the bushes into our garden which backed onto the park. Any gardeners in the locality (and they had a small shed, in which they smoked and drank tea, positioned dangerously close) would curse and threaten me for treading a path through their shrubbery, but I continued to do it and continued to escape any of the threatened retribution.

One of my clearest memories of the grammar school is my first chemistry lesson. I was taught chemistry by a pleasant fat Welshman called Mr. Owen. I believe he intended to impress us in our first encounter with him. As far as I was concerned, he succeeded.

The chemistry lab was arranged as a series of blackened benches at which the boys worked and, at right angles to them, a demonstration bench at which the teacher would conduct especially dangerous or complex experiments. As we entered the room Mr. Owen stood behind the demonstration bench. *"Gather round boys"*, he said in his deep Welsh accent. He pointed to a brick which had been placed on his bench. On it was a small conical pile of a dark grey powder. Later we learned it was gunpowder.

"Now boys," he said, *"watch this little heap of harmless looking powder"*. He applied a lighted wax taper to it. There was a bright flash and a dense cloud of smoke. As it slowly cleared the stout figure of Mr. Owen was revealed. Through the haze he appeared to be dancing about, waving his hands in the air. As the smoke continued to disperse it became apparent that his white lab coat was on fire and he was beating at the flames in a somewhat desperate manner. Eventually he doused them with some water from a large conical flask. He had intended to impress us. He had done so beyond his expectations. I developed an immediate interest in chemistry.

My father arranged the school timetables and, in so doing, ensured that he never taught me himself. I did however, have a series of interesting teachers and some very good ones too.

My first form master in Form 1A (Room 19) was Joe Higginbottom. He was small, had slick Brylcreamed hair and wore horn-rimmed spectacles. He was very keen on gardening. As punishments, rather than hand out lines or detentions he would demand essays on selected horticultural subjects, and woe betide you if they were inadequately researched. I was a less than angelic little boy. The culture of carrots and subsequently of carnations are two topics I can still recall with some clarity.

Mr. Foulds, who I don't think had a Christian name, taught me physics. He was a gaunt, somewhat daunting figure. He closed his eyes for considerable periods from time to time giving rise to debate as to whether he was asleep. A chalk box on the bench in front of him marked *"give generously to the blind"* certainly escaped his attention for several weeks.

83

I shall pass over the teachers I didn't like for some, I know, are still alive and well. I wish neither to offend them nor to have them sue me.

I shall pass on accordingly to Reg Moss who, my father having carefully avoided me, taught me French. He was a good teacher, bouncy and energetic with a great sense of humour. His problem lay in an inability to pronounce the letter R, something of a handicap in mastering an authentic French accent. Rolling your W's just isn't the same.

I had always had an interest biology but, in the 1950s: it wasn't an option until the Sixth form. There I studied botany and zoology and was taught both subjects very well by *'Rocky Wilson'*. He led me to develop such an interest in the subject that it formed the basis for much of my subsequent career. His slow but careful and thorough approach suited me well. Surrounded by drooping plants, partially dissected dogfish, rats, frogs and earthworms and smelling strongly of formaldehyde, he remained calm and unruffled telling us of Darwin's theory of evolution, Mendelian genetics and the inevitable ultimate triumph of socialism.

The Oak Street premises were an important part of the Co-operative Society's empire. Above the shop were offices and large rooms, used on a daily basis for weddings and funerals. On the left is the clog shop. The tower of Oak Street Congregational Chapel watches over the scene in the early years of the century.

1 - 2 - 4 - 2 - 5

Edna Beach recalls something from her childhood in the 1940s.

My mother had an order book
And in it she would write
All the things she wanted
From the Co-op on Friday night.

You didn't get a trolley and
go round and serve yourself.
You had to ask a man for it
Or point to it on the shelf.

Cheese and butter were on a slab,
biscuits in shiny tins,
Sugar was weighed in little bags
And flour was in bins.

There'd be tokens for your pinta
and dolly blue for your clothes
And all the different aromas
Would mingle up your nose.

The counter was of dark brown wood,
The floor was wood as well
And when you opened the shop door
You'd hear the tinkle of a bell.

You had to stand and wait your turn
But there would be a seat
So that the older folks could take
The weight from off their feet.

The coupons in the ration books
Didn't go very far
Because you couldn't have just anything
When England was at war.

When my mother gave the man
Her little order book
He'd get the things she wanted
And what a time it took.

Then it was all totted up -
Sometimes he'd do it twice.
There were no girls on check-outs
On tills that gave the price.

Now the Co-op they had a 'divi'
What they paid you now and then,
And you had to say a number
Whenever you 'bought in'.

So when everything was packed in bags
My big moment did arrive.
I'd look at the man and I would say
'One two four two five'.

'PRINCE WITH A PIECE OF LEATHER'

by Gerry Wolstenholme

In his heyday Hedley Verity, one of England's greatest ever slow left-arm bowlers, was known as the *'Prince with a Piece of Leather'*. It is perhaps not fully appreciated that Accrington Cricket Club can take some credit for his development. He was professional at the Cemetery Ground in 1927 and although the young Yorkshireman did not have an outstanding season, he undoubtedly polished his already developing talents and learnt much about the professional side of the game of cricket.

No less a personage than the great Yorkshire and England all-rounder George Hirst recommended Verity to Accrington when the committee approached him to find them a *'good professional'*. Verity was not quite 22 but he had already made his name as an opening bat and spin bowler with Rawdon and latterly Horsforth Hall Park, where in the 1926 season he had won the Yorkshire Council bowling prize with 62 wickets at just nine runs each.

Accrington, in their Jubilee Year, were delighted to sign him as professional and, amongst other favourable remarks, the local press reported *'...he is only 21 years of age and has therefore, a long career in front of him ...he promises to be a very popular professional.'*

With favourable reviews ringing in his ears, the gladiator arrived. His introduction to Lancashire League cricket was at Bacup and many Accrington folk travelled to the game to see the new boy in action. Despite bowling Bacup out for 106, Verity starring with 5-48, Accrington lost by four runs. Opening the batting, Verity top-scored with 34 made in an hour and it was reported that he showed *'sound defence'* which was combined with *'an ability to hit freely on both sides of the wicket'* but the team were 102 all out. His five wicket bowling performance prompted the comment *'when there is life in the pitch his deliveries will prove somewhat troublesome to batsmen.'*

Verity performed moderately well with the ball in the next few games but then came the low point of his, and the team's, season. It was against the 1926 wooden-spoonists Lowerhouse. Verity bowled admirably and with 6-40 he was instrumental in bowling Lowerhouse out for just 83, but this proved to be 74 runs too many for Accrington who in turn were dismissed for a measly nine! This included a no-ball by Lowerhouse professional Fred Webster and a top score of five by Sproule. There were seven ducks including Verity who was caught behind after surviving for three overs. Ironically, three weeks earlier, Lowerhouse themselves had been bowled out for nine by Bacup but for this performance, the *'Accrington Observer'* could only report under the headline *'Accrington's Humiliation!'*

Accrington continued their up-and-down season and Verity took wickets in most games although at mid-season, the *'Accrington Observer'* was reporting *'the one disappointment has been the lack of success on the part of Verity.'* By the end of June, the rumours were rife that the club were seeking a new professional for the following season. The Committee eventually confirmed the rumour and added *'It may be that with more experience Verity will develop into a fine all-round cricketer but the Lancashire League demands professionals of proven ability.'*

Losing more than winning was the story of the rest of the Accrington season but Verity, a young professional carrying a weak side, did his best and finished the season with 67 wickets at the respectable average of 13.13 runs each. Shuffling up and down the order from number one to number seven, his batting suffered and he made only 95 runs at 5.27, a most disappointing return for a man who later made over 5,000 first-class runs.

Hedley Verity spent the next three seasons as professional at Middleton and in the last of them he made his debut for Yorkshire. The Hedley Verity story then took on a new twist as he became one of Yorkshire and England's greatest ever left-arm bowlers. His performance of 10-10 against Nottinghamshire at Headingley in 1932 will never be bettered and he undoubtedly would have gone on to add to his 1,956 first-class wickets if World War Two had not cruelly taken his life. He was mortally wounded when leading his company of Green Howards in a night attack near Catania and died later in an Italian hospital.

Sir Stanley Jackson captured the nation's mood with an apt comment *'Verity was a man tremendously respected by everyone, and a fine fellow. To put it simply, he did everything a man could possibly do for his country.'* Even though he was not tremendously successful in his year at Accrington, there is no doubt that he tried to do everything he could for the town's cricket team.

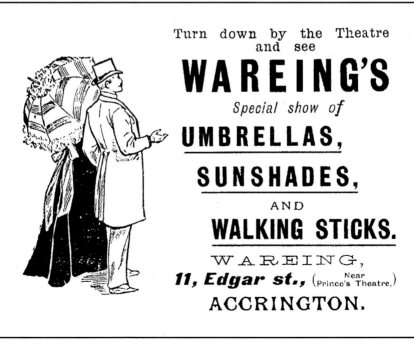

TWO-LEG
David Airey

'Two-leg, umpire, if you please',
Stop breathing quite so fast.
Concentrate and play it straight
- This wicket's thinly grassed.

Tell yourself you're here for hours
- Just like it was last week.
We know you only hit three runs
But what a sound technique.

'Thank you, umpire - three to come
And hat-trick ball? - I see.
'Round the wicket'. Don't be glum.
A century for me.

I'll rent him fore and drive him firm
Then hook him, given a chance.
And if his line and length should stray
Well, round the leg I'll glance.

'You're going to field right by the bat?
With a helmet - oh, I see!'
If he's going to bowl as quick as that
You'd better lend it me.

Thank God I thought to wear a box
To guard my bits and bobs.
Not over-keen on knocks and shocks
Or digits when they throbs.

He's taken five for twenty-one?
'Cos he's working early shift
And he's found a spot just off length
That's giving quite a lift.

Does he think it's really sense
To place all ten behind?
Leaving all that open space!
What's going through his mind?

Well - here he comes!
It's easy when you watch it to the bat
Don't let him hear your knocking knees
Just give him tit for tat.

Good grief! He is a big 'un!
He must stand six foot six!
And he's built just like an out house
Of steel and Nori bricks.

'Sorry skip! Regret to say
I never saw the thing!
Yes - I'm fully conscious, yet
My head it don't half sting'.

'When this red haze has passed away
And when I've had a piddle
I'll contemplate the benefits
Of taking leg and middle'.

ACCRINGTON'S CINEMAS IN 1950

Frank Watson

It is hard to believe that Accrington in 1995 does not even have one cinema, yet in 1950 it supported six - and one theatre, the Hippodrome. In 1950 it was possible to see a different film every night of the week with very little travelling, as all six cinemas were located within a few hundred yards of each other surrounding the town centre.

Accrington's six cinemas in 1950 listed in pecking order.

1. *Odeon* on Broadway.
2. *Princess* on Edgar Street.
3. *Palace* on Whalley Road.
4. *Empire* on Edgar Street.
5. *Ritz* on Church Street.
6. *King's Hall* on Whalley Road.

Cinemas, like most things in life that compete with each other, had what could be termed a *'pecking order'* according to their popularity with the general public. The Odeon was number one, and the King's Hall definitely number six. Compared to present day football clubs, the Odeon would have been Premier League, and the King's Hall a non-league club, or put another way, at the Odeon they employed very attractive usherettes, whilst the King's Hall employed a chucker-out not renowned for his handsome profile or diplomatic manner.

If one was prepared to travel within the present boundaries of Hyndburn then one could choose from another nine cinemas:- Palladium, Empire and Palace in Oswaldtwistle, Queen's in Church, Star and Rex in Clayton, Savoy in Rishton, Palace and Grand in Great Harwood. By 1960, four of Accrington's cinemas had closed.

The Origins of Cinemas in Accrington

Just after the turn of the century, silent films were shown in local buildings that were not purpose built for this new medium. The first recorded event of moving pictures being shown in Accrington was in 1902 when a travelling company known as the *'Edison Animated Picture Company'* leased the Town Hall for this purpose. Prior to this, the company had recorded on film the funeral of Alderman Whittaker, and scenes of employees leaving the works of Howard & Bullough's, which they included in their normal programme to help stimulate more interest in this new medium.

Dowry Street Picture Palace had the distinction of being the first permanent picture palace in Accrington, being opened to the public on Monday, 28th February, 1910. The actual building dated back to 1860, and had formerly been a small engineering works. The proud manager of this new enterprise was a Mr. Witham. The seats were described as *'a comfortable tip-up type'* all being laid out on the ground floor. This first cinema could accommodate somewhere between four and five hundred people with the cheapest seats priced at tuppence.

It closed as a cinema sometime during 1916 and most of its customers then switched their patronage to the King's Hall Cinema.

King's Hall. In all probability this was the second cinema to open in Accrington, but the actual date that this former Methodist Chapel opened as a cinema does not appear to have been recorded in the local press. A photograph of a procession to celebrate the

Coronation of King George V in June 1911 clearly shows the building as a cinema.

It has been documented that its original owners as a cinema were the Weisker brothers, two former German waiters who had prior to opening this cinema in Accrington built up a small chain of cinemas in Liverpool. It was originally known as the *Picturedrome*, but it changed its name to the more familiar *King's Hall* in 1915. A Mr. Thomas Haworth who became the proprietor in 1913 was responsible for introducing talkies at this cinema in 1931. He was superseded by a Mr. Hammer in 1934 who ran the cinema until it finally closed on the 3rd January 1959. At its closure the top price seats for an adult on the balcony was still only one shilling. The building was demolished in May 1962 to be replaced by the present Lloyds Bank.

Although it only had two official names during its life as a cinema, it had a number of unofficial ones due to its habit if showing mainly cowboy films and the unhygienic conditions inside the building, e.g.: *The Ranch, The Corral, The Bug-Hut, The Laugh and Scratch, The Flea-Pit* and *The Fleck-Oyle*. There does not seem to be an official statistic of how many people this cinema could accommodate. This could be due to the fact that at one time the front few rows were benches, and youngsters were packed on at one end and then slid across until some of them fell off at the other end, especially during the cheap and popular Saturday Matinees, known locally as the *'tuppenny-rush'*. In the late 1940s I can personally remember collecting six empty one pound jam jars, which I then washed and cleaned, before returning them to a local grocers shop to gain six pennies that then enabled me to sample once more the delights of this old cinema.

When the film projector broke down, as it often did in the early fifties, the catcall to the projectionist used to be *'light another candle'*, in an oblique reference to the low intensity of the light from the early projection equipment still in use at this time. Stamping of feet on the wooden floor whilst waiting for the film to restart kept Ken Wilkinson, the resident chucker-out, fully employed trying to restore order.

Empire. This was the third cinema to open, but it had the distinction of being the first purpose-built one when it opened on Wednesday, 12th April, 1911.

It was built on a site next to the Princess Theatre that was previously occupied by a temperance hotel and three shops. The auditorium was about 51 feet by 47 feet with seating for 500 downstairs and another 300 in the balcony. The exterior was built of brick with glazed terra-cotta dressings. It was built by a Mr. Wilson who in 1912 also took over the Princess Theatre next door, but in 1915 he sold both to Messrs. Wood & Lyall of Liverpool. It eventually closed as a cinema in 1960, but was reopened as a Bingo-Hall in 1961. After a complete refurbishment it was reopened as a cinema in February 1965, and renamed the *New Princess* to replace the original Princess Theatre that had burnt down in November 1964.

It finally closed as a cinema to the general public on the 13th April 1974, but then had another short lease of life as a cinema showing special films just to the local ethnic community. Its only real claim to fame was that it was one of the few cinemas with two cosy corners, one on each side at the back of the auditorium, which were very popular with courting couples in 1950.

Palace. This was the second purpose-built cinema, and was opened on 22nd September 1915, to become Accrington's fourth cinema. It was built with a pronounced rise in the floor on the body of the hall, and each row of seats in the balcony was on a separate tier.

This was to ensure that each of the 750 seats had a clear view of the screen. A Mr. Warburton was the conductor of the orchestra when the cinema first opened. In 191 the owners decided that an organ would be a useful addition, and might even replace the orchestra. Jardine's, the organ makers, produced an orchestral organ which was the first in the country to be specifically designed for the cinema.

With the introduction of talkies the organ became surplus to requirements, and was sold to Hapton Methodist Church in 1934. The Palace had just one cosy corner at the back of the auditorium. The Palace closed as a cinema on the 12th October 1960, but the building is still in use in 1995 as a retail outlet.

Princess. The original *'Princess Theatre'* became the fifth cinema in Accrington when it was converted to show silent films in 1920. It continued to show films until 1926 when it reverted back to its original role as a theatre for about three years. It reopened as a cinema showing talkies in 1929. The only time it was used as a theatre after 1929 was during 1962/63 when Accrington Amateurs staged their annual productions there.

The site if the Princess was bought by the Ormerod family with the intention of building a warehouse on the site. They encountered considerable opposition when they decided to build a theatre. As originally constructed, the Princess Theatre provided accommodation for about 1400 people when it opened on the 6th March 1882. By 1950 many structural alterations had taken place making it into a cosy cinema, well patronised by the public, but one had to take care to avoid the seats directly behind the supporting pillars at both sides of the pit and circle.

It was still in regular use as a cinema in November 1964 when the building was almost totally destroyed by a fire that left Accrington Amateurs homeless.

Its claim to fame is that Charlie Chaplin appeared on its stage playing the part of Billy the pageboy in a touring production of Sherlock Holmes for one week in February 1905, when he was only fifteen. The drama critic of the *'Accrington Observer'* at the time summed up Chaplin's performance in a few words: *'Charles Chaplin makes a good servant (Billy) of the great detective'.*

Picture House; *The Ritz.* The *'Picture House'* was the third purpose-built cinema in Accrington, opening on Saturday, 7th January, 1922. Before the building could be erected on a site in Church Street buildings of a not very pretentious character (slums) had to be demolished. It retained its original name until 10th December 1934 when it was renamed *The Ritz.* The new Ritz Ballroom and Restaurant which was erected near the cinema had its official opening on the 13th December 1934, and was no doubt the main reason for the change in name.

Safety was high on the list of purpose-built cinemas due to the highly inflammable nature of the large reels of film. The operating room was built of steel and concrete entirely cut off from the rest of the building. The cinema was lit by electricity, but the emergency lighting was gas in case the electricity supply failed. At its opening it was noted in the local press that *'the external appearance of the building is not very impressive'*, and this was never changed during its time as a cinema. Whether this had any bearing on it being the first purpose-built cinema in Accrington to close is open to conjecture. It showed its last film on 2nd August 1958. The building was eventually taken over by Barnes as an extension to their premises next door and many of the original features of this former cinema can still be seen as one wanders round this furniture shop in 1995.

Regal; Odeon. The *'Regal'* was the fourth purpose-built cinema in Accrington, opened on the former site of Myers Stables. It was opened on Monday 12th April 1937 with the price of seats ranging from six pence up to one shilling and three pence. It could accommodate 950 in the auditorium and 350 in the circle.

It was renamed the *'Odeon'* in April 1945 when it became part of a large group of cinemas owned by Oscar Deutch hence the reason for the new name which stood for **Oscar Deutch Entertains Our Nation.** In 1950 the manager, when on duty, always wore an evening suit with black bow tie. It also employed a commissionaire who wore a long maroon coat and matching trousers. The coat was decorated with gilt braid and gold buttons plus a matching maroon hat. In 1950 this illusion of sartorial elegance had the nickname of *'Custard Lips'*. The onerous duties he performed outside the entrance to the cinema was to control the large number of patrons at peak times in orderly queues, and to occasionally shout out instructions, e.g.: *"Room in the circle pass straight in"*, (these were the dearest seats). The cinema also had its own cafe downstairs, and a restaurant upstairs. In 1950, the restaurant had white linen cloths on each table whilst in Accrington at this time most kitchen tables were still covered with newspapers during the week with table cloths reserved for weekends or special occasions. The **Odeon Saturday Morning Club** was formed just after the Second World War to cater for children only, and it continued for many years becoming so popular that police were detailed to be on duty outside the cinema to deal with over a thousand children as they spilled out onto Broadway at the end of the film. The Saturday Morning Club even had its own song which we all sang at the start aided by the words being projected onto the screen, and a bouncing ball skipping along the top of the words in time to the music. In its heyday in the early 1950s the best job was carried out by the under-manager, who in the large foyer upstairs behind the circle had the task of inspecting the standard of dress of the uniformed usherettes as they stood in line everyday before they went on duty. The Odeon did not have a cosy corner, but in order to cater for the local courting couples a number of seats in the circle were known as 'doubles' because they had no armrest in the middle.

If one could not afford the entrance price in 1950 to this up-market cinema, then one had to arrange with a couple of one's friends that they would open the emergency exit down the steps just below the Gent's toilets at a prearranged time. To accomplish the delicate task of gaining entry to the cinema undetected it required two people already inside the cinema to co-operate. One had to gently open the emergency doors and then close them quietly whilst the second person held the curtains at the entrance to the Gent's to stop them billowing out into the auditorium, which immediately alerted the usherettes that the emergency exit had been opened to allow non-paying patrons to enter. (I believe the unofficial record was for two males going to the toilets and twelve returning)

The cinema was renamed the *'Classic'* in December 1967 when it was taken over by another company. In October 1973 it was again taken over by a group known as Unit 4 who converted it into a multi screen cinema. Even though it only had three screens it retained the name of Unit 4 until it eventually closed on the 23rd March 1990 to allow the site to be redeveloped.

The Hippodrome. The *'Hippodrome Theatre'* located at the bottom of Ellison Street has not been included in this article because in 1950 it was in use as a theatre for live shows. It only operated as a cinema during the late 1920s and most of the 1930s before reverting mainly to live theatre. The Hippodrome was the venue for the first full length talking picture to be screened in Accrington on 29th August 1929. The film was *'The Donovan Affair'*, advertised as the first one hundred percent talking movie. In the next two years many musicians found themselves out of work as, by 1931, all the cinemas had installed the new projection equipment to enable them to show talkies. The King's Hall was the last local cinema to switch.

(Accrington Library Local History Collection)

THE KING'S HALL

Fred Barrett

The *'King's Hall'* was a dilapidated cinema situated at the junction of Whalley Road and Peel Street, the site now being occupied by a branch of Lloyds Bank. It had obviously been built originally as a place of worship, but, as a cinema, catered for worship of a different kind - that of adventure and excitement, specialising in *'blood and thunder'* films. To us young boys of that era, Saturday afternoon at the King's Hall was the highlight of the week, and provided us with a main topic of conversation for the following week. When one walked through its doors, one was transported back to the Edwardian period, bare board floors, form seats, still illuminated by gas mantles around the walls, each with its own long chains to turn them on and off. The incidents in the following reminiscences occurred on any (or every) Saturday, and the mayhem and organised chaos, which was the King's Hall, was responsible for some of the happiest days of our childhood.

MEMORIES OF THE KING'S HALL (1936-1942)

Kings Oyle? Eeeh, id were a gradely place,
Just thinkin' o' gooin'd leet up thee face.
Set-day afternoon, that's when we went theer,
An tha hed to be soon if tha wanted a cheear.
There were forms deauwn at front, fer them as come late,
An they rocked awl ooer t'place, like a jelly on a plate.

Eawtside, The King's Hall it said were its reight name,
But id were called other things which meant summat t'same,
T'Flea-Pit, Ranch, but to most of us Bug-Hut,
showed pirates wi soords, whose throoats'd geet cut,
Ceawboys and Indians, sowjers an awl,
Tha could see em on a placard, eawtside, up on't wall.

Ah'd hev to cadge twopence fro' off mi mam,
"When tha're crossin' t'main rooad, watch eawt fer tram!"
If tha hedn't two pennies, tha could allus get in,
Fer a penny a jar that jam ud bin in.
Tha'd goo up stooan steps, to t'paybox at top,
An owd woman sat theear, wi hair like a mop.

Then through t'blanket curtains, booath ripped an awl dusty,
An into t'front stalls, smelling reight musty.
Wallpaper were pealin an' t'gas leets splutterin,
Kids'd bi sheawtin, an th'owder uns mutterin.
Tha'd ged owd of a cheear, if any were theear,
If nod, then a saddle on t'forms, but they were a bit near.

Then owd Bob'd come in, wi big tash an flat cap,
He'd turn gas leets eawt, wi pullin t'chain tap,
An Robin, wi muffler, he'd come reaund an he'd sheawt,
If yo dond shut thad noise, Ah'll cob yo awl eawt.
T'fost picture'd start, id'd flicker an jump,
Then a form'd tip ooer, to hit flooer wi a thump.
They'd awl ged up an start wi their sheawtin'
An Robin'd come, an give 'em a cleawtin'.

When th'adverts were on, tha'd ged deawn t'front, it tha were able,
Owd Bob'd set his stall eawt on a card table,
They said he'd bin killed in Coventry blitz,
But, neaw, heaw could he,...he were theear, selling crisps.
Then t'serial'd start, there'd be a to-do,

We'd a waited sin last week to see what come true
Tha'd think, Neaw, heaw did id finish?, tha could'nt think on,
Then, Oh aye, they awl geet blown up, deead to a mon.

Th'hero'd come on, Ah think he were called Tom,
He'd hev to bi sharp, when t'villains lit bomb,
Neaw, they'd bi reight theear, thad'd bi just were they war,
When t'bomb went off reight under their car
But, this week, sithee, he'd turn off deawn bi thad lake,
An awl kids'd bi sheawtin, "Sheeeee, whad a fake."
Then Bob an Robin'd come flyin through t'dooar,
As hundreds o' clogs ud start stampin on t'flooer.

Somebody deawn't front'd throw a stink bomb on t'flooer,
Bob'd grab him an throw him eawt, reight through t'dooer.
An oooh, whad a stink, id'd bi awl ooer t'place,
Ah can see t'look neaw on everybody's face.
Ah can remember another mon, gooin eawt of his mind,
He'd hed chewin gum stuck on his heead, fro behind.
It served him reight, he thowt he were toff,
His Mam'd bi awl neet geddin thad lot off.

After t'end, tha'd get eawt quick if tha could,
'Cos they'd play t'King, an then theear tha'd bi stood.
An gooin hooam , crossin t'market, we'd loiter an linger,
Playin ceawboys, shootin guns, wi pointin us finger.
But, tha'd bi hooam fer five, if tha hed any fear,
'Cos if tha weren't, tha'd end up wi what's called a thick ear.

An neaw, after fifty years or sooa,
Th'owd Bug-Huts gone, its nod theear any mooar,
Kids can wetch ceawboys, Tarzan or Mickey Meause,
Witheawt even gooin eawtside o'their heause.
But to me, lookin back, Ah sometimes thinks Aaaay,
After gooin t'Bug-Hut, watchin TV's like suppin cowd tae.

ACCRINGTON'S AUGUST FAIR

Martin Baggoley

There were two fairs held annually in Victorian Accrington, the first of which took place in early May. This was the cattle fair, at which cattle and other livestock were exhibited, bought and sold. The second was that held in early August, and although it began in a small way, it developed into one of the great occasions for the town's population, eagerly anticipated by men and women, young and old, and all social classes.

On the Thursday following the first Friday in August, the scholars of St. James's Sunday School had traditionally held their annual procession through the town to celebrate the Dedication Festival of St. James. In 1825, a small number of enterprising Accringtonians erected their stalls outside the Bay Horse, on Church Street, to provide the scholars and spectators with refreshments. As the fair grew in importance, Thursday remained the opening day, heralded by the ringing of the church bells.

Other Accrington Sunday schools began to walk at Fair time, and the processions were to remain a feature of the fair for many years. With scholars in their best clothing, and with their many banners flying proudly, it must have been a magnificent sight. This is clear from a description of the 1869 processions, for which the Sunday schools of St. James's and St. John's combined. 1,600 marched, taking half an hour to pass any point. At the front was the Accrington Volunteers Rifle Band, followed by the vicar and church wardens of St. James's church, who led their scholars, whilst the scholars from St. John's were accompanied by a drum and fife band. They walked along Wellington Street, Abbey Street, Plantation Street to Avenue Parade, making their way to the home of Mr. Steiner, where they sang a selection of hymns, which included, *'My Sunday School'*, *'Teach us the Song'*, *'Rejoice the Lord is King'* and *'The Tender Lambs'*. At the end, each youngster received a bun and tuppence. On the same day, 700 scholars from New Jerusalem Sunday School, walked to the market area; 450 from the Primitive Methodist Sunday School marched to the house of their pastor in Birch Street; 400 from the Wesley Sabbath School, and 300 from Bethel Street Sunday School also walked through the town.

As the railways expanded, each Sunday school usually arranged a day trip over fair time. Popular destinations included Manchester's Belle Vue Gardens, Morecambe Bay, Liverpool, Windermere, Southport and Blackpool. In 1859 some of the excursionists to York were severely criticised for taking the opportunity of attending a public hanging. Despite the popularity of these excursions, in 1871 the Sunday schools boycotted the Lancashire and Yorkshire Railway Company's trips because of increases to many of the fares for the excursions from 3s. 6d. by a further sixpence. Instead, the scholars held a great gala in Barn Field, attended by several thousands.

The fair soon began to attract large crowds and it was not only Accringtonians who would attend. The mills and other workplaces of Church and Oswaldtwistle closed for the whole of the weekend, specifically because of Accrington Fair. Accounts from the Accrington press between 1860 and 1880 provide marvellous descriptions of the stalls, booths, rides and shows that people flocked to see. There were roundabouts, swinging boats, hobby horses, shooting galleries, and the ample figure of Henry VIII attracted passers-by into an exhibition of wax figures. A pair of clowns enticed revellers into a marionette show, and there were boxing booths, in which fairgoers could take on visiting toughs. Machines we

St. James' Church and the Bay Horse Hotel from Warner Street in the early years of the century. This was where the street market was held before the Market Hall was built.
(*Accrington Library Local History Collection*)

now take for granted were new and exciting to our Victorian ancestors, so weighing machines, those which were blown into to measure lung power, and strikers which registered the power of a blow struck by a large hammer caused great interest.

Freak shows were immensely popular and for the entrance fee of one penny, one might see the fat woman known as *'The Lancashire Beauty'*, *'The Norfolk giant'*, a giant baby, a spotted man, a living skeleton or Tommy Dodd and his wife, *'two of the smallest people in the world'*. An ever popular attraction was the half man - half woman, who was an individual who had carefully developed muscles and other body features on just one side of the body to give the illusion of two genders in one body. A travelling menagerie provided the opportunity for many to see for the first time the world's wild and exotic animals. In the early 1870s a skating rink was erected with entrance costing sixpence, a similar sum being charged for the hire of skates.

Cheapjacks who hawked cheap trinkets were a regular and noisy feature. Stallholders sold a wide range of wares, such as baskets, jewellery, toys and pottery. In 1870, one observer noted the gullibility of some of the fairgoers, when he witnessed a woman hawking purses for one shilling, after pretending each one contained a half crown. Refreshments were provided by stallholders selling soft drinks, hot peas, gingerbread, Eccles cakes, ice cream, fruit, nuts and in 1888 we find the first mention in the press account of a chip potato stall. With so much crammed into the centre of the town, inevitably there were problems, which persisted until the market grounds opened later in the century. For instance, in 1862, Richard Pilkington, a hobby horse proprietor was brought before the magistrates for causing an obstruction in Dutton Street. His contraption blocked the windows of the office of solicitor George Barlow, who had to board them up to prevent them from being broken. He was forced to close his office for the fair's duration, and issued a summons against Pilkington. The magistrates found in Barlow's favour and stated that the defendant was liable to pay a fine of 40s., but as it was fair time, they would make an allowance and only fine him 7s. 6d.

Drunkenness was a perennial problem, and magistrates were kept extremely busy by drunkards. In 1876, Joseph Clayton was fined 5s. for being drunk and riotous, as were Henry Pollard, and William Grimshaw. Another man, William Livesey, described in court as a cripple, was locked up for a similar offence but was discharged having promised to leave town. In 1881, Anne Carey, an 'old offender' was committed to prison for one month with hard labour for being drunk and disorderly. In 1889, James Martin was seen by Police Superintendent Campbell, to be drunk and indecently exposing himself to large numbers of women at the fair, for which he was fined 10s., or 14 days in prison in default.

The fair attracted large numbers of ne'er-do-wells, who packed into Accrington's lodging houses, the most notorious of which were those in Duke Street, kept by the infamous German Jemmy. In these dens, where a night's bed cost just a few pennies, thieves, pickpockets, prostitutes and cardsharps would stay. Some were unsuccessful in their endeavours and ended up in front of the magistrates. In 1858, Mary Marsden, a prostitute, was arrested in Broad Oak Lane by PC Swift and was committed to the Preston House of Correction for fourteen days. In 1870, Eliza Hartley, a prostitute who had travelled from Rochdale for the duration of the fair was arrested on Church Street, and was also sent to the House of Correction. In 1873, the police spotted a gang of pickpockets but prevented any offences by keeping them under constant observation. In the same year, a cardsharp was arrested, and it was discovered he was also wanted by the Barnsley police.

However, it was not just offenders such as these who found themselves in court. In 1867, Abraham Hughes, who worked at Wilkinson's printworks in Clayton-le-Moors, was charged with absenting himself from work without permission. He had asked his manager for time off to attend Accrington fair, but this had been refused. Nevertheless, he stayed off work for the fair's duration. His employers took him to court, and much to the annoyance of their solicitor, who argued for a severe deterrent penalty, the magistrates showed a great deal of leniency. As he was willing to return to work, and as it was fair time, the magistrates simply discharged him upon payment of costs. The argument that followed in open court between the solicitor and the magistrates led to the former receiving a severe reprimand.

By the end of the nineteenth century, Accrington fair was in decline. The number of Sunday schools marching at the fair had gradually dwindled, until they had all opted to do so at Whitsuntide. A more ordered and disciplined society was emerging, and raucous events were increasingly discouraged. One correspondent to the *'Accrington Times'* in 1890, described the local fair as a *'carnival of vice'* - which lured the town's youth into *'a life of drunkenness and crime'*. Furthermore, the workplaces of Accrington had traditionally ceased work on the Thursday evening of the fair, and resumed operations the following Tuesday, but this period was gradually extended as the years passed, so that many employers closed down for the whole of the following week. Thus, Accrington's traditional wakes holiday came into being and more and more Accringtonians left to spend their holidays at the seaside. The great days of Accrington August Fair had passed by, and with them one of the great events in the lives of our ancestors.

The Market, Accrington.

The Market Hall, which put paid to the street market. This is a postcard view taken in the early years of the century.

99

T'STANLEY: SOME FACTS

In 1907, Accrington Stanley Football Club, an association of football enthusiasts, became a company. The £1,000 capital was divided into £1 shares. There were four directors:- John Harwood (30 shares), Whalley House, Whalley Road; gentleman; Richard Watson (14 shares), 139 Avenue Parade; mechanic; John Thomas Whittaker (14 shares), Manchester Road; gentleman; James Henry Lupton (14 shares), Owen Street; grocer; William Edwards (5 shares), Ormerod Street; labourer; and George Somerville (10 shares), Owen Street; electrical engineer.

On 8th September 1921, the company became a public company with a nominal value of £5,000 in £1 shares.

On 6th March 1962, board members, George Clarkson (Chairman), Lawrence Eddleston (Sec.), Jack Daniels and Stanley Armitage instructed the manager, John Wigglesworth, to tender resignation from the Football League. Despite an almost immediate withdrawl of that resignation letter from Sir William Cocker, the club President, Alan Hardaker, the Secretary, kicked Stanley out of the League. Thus Accrington achieved the distinction of losing two teams from the Football League, as Accrington F.C. (Th'owd Reds) left in 1893.

The club continued to play in the Lancashire Combination and the West Lancashire League, but on 13th November 1963, the Inland Revenue presented a petition to the High Court. They were looking to get blood out of a stone, as the court heard that the club's estimated total deficiency was £63,688, while assets were worth just £708. The Official Receiver blamed the failure and insolvency on the directors' mismanagement, as they had overspent on ground and other improvements without taking into account the team's performance. A liquidator was appointed. *'On, Stanley On'*, became *'Gone, Stanley Gone'*.

In the mid-1950s, in t'Stanley's golden (goalden?) years, Harry Crossley, editor of the *'Accrington Observer'*, wrote a stirring song entitled *'On, Stanley, On'*. He didn't claim to have invented the phrase, and it had probably been in use for many years by that time, but he certainly didn't know of its literary origin. Those three words are the last spoken by Marmion in Sir Walter Scott's epic poem of that name about the Battle of Flodden Field. The Stanley referred to was Edward, son of the first Earl of Derby. He was Sheriff of Lancashire in 1485 and, in 1513, commanded a large Lancashire and Cheshire contingent at Flodden. Marmion was referring to the Cheshire men as 'Chester' when he shouted *'Charge, Chester, charge. On, Stanley, on'*.

T'Stanley's place in the record books is assured, if only for something which happened in a game they played at Wolverhampton on the afternoon of Monday 14th September 1891 before 3,000 witnesses. Just after half-time, already one goal down, a Stanley full-back *'acted as a goalkeeper'* (said the Birmingham Daily Gazette reporter) *'...and the new rule which gives a free kick to the attacking side with no one but the defending goalkeeper in front was enforced'*. This new rule being referred to was what we now call a penalty. It was the first one to be awarded in a league match. Wanderers scored from the spot, and ended up winning 5-nil.

BILL PARKY: MR. ACCRINGTON STANLEY

The story of the departure from the Football League, in 1962, of Accrington Stanley, has often been told. It is worthwhile to record the rebirth of the name, in particular the action of one man in effecting the return.

William 'Bill' Parkinson had watched t'Stanley from the terraces since 1934, when he was a ten-year-old. When that fateful day arrived in 1962, he was a 'regular' at Peel Park, and in fact owned a couple of dozen shares. He was in business in the town as a furniture remover.

For six years following the team's demise, Bill watched football locally on the town's playing fields. Some games featured a team called 'Accrington Stanley Reserves'.

In 1968, now a councillor for Milnshaw Ward, Bill called a public meeting in Bold Street Working Men's Club to test support for a football club which would wear the town's name. The meeting was packed to the doors. They learned that the old ground had passed to the control of Peel Park School. Fired with enthusiasm, Bill, on behalf of the meeting, applied to the Corporation for land which could be used as a football ground.

Two council-owned areas were offered: Arden Hall, which wasn't suitable, and some badly drained land behind the Crown Inn, Whalley Road. The latter was accepted at a nominal rent of £3 per annum, conditional upon there being no sales of alcohol there. Bill put his own head on the block by guaranteeing that he would be personally responsible for any debts incurred by the newly-formed club in their first twelve months. Accrington Stanley (1968) had been born, and in June 1970 was accepted as a league member by the Lancashire Combination.

The period from 1968 to 1970 was spent by Bill and a group of enthusiasts in fund-raising; selling raffle tickets and the like. Each hundred pounds raised was spent on the ground and its facilities.

The team's weekly wages bill for the first season was £25. The manager, Jimmy Hincksman, got £5, three part-time professionals got £5 each, and the other players ten shillings each. Bill remembers the period well, *"Some weeks I had to pay it out of my own pocket"*. The first game in their new red and white (what else?) strip was at the Crown Ground against Formby Town. A thousand fans watched the 2-1 victory. The finances were assisted not by sponsorship but by local firms giving donations and advertising in the programme.

In the following season, t'Stanley won both the League and Combination Cup.

Bill speaks in praise of his friends at the club and in the town who helped put Accrington on the football map of England once again. He insists that many people share the credit. He gave up the chairmanship after a few years but continues to be interested and supportive of the club. He had a business to run, and took part in the business of the town. He was the last Mayor of Accrington in 1973/4, but returned as Mayor of Hyndburn in 1987/8.

Speaking in 1994 from his home in Stanley (where else?) Street, Bill used the present, not the past, tense when he said, *"I have a passionate feeling for Accrington Stanley"*. He is modest about his part in the rebirth, and quick to heap praise on a team. Not the footballers, but the team of workers which included himself and Jimmy Hincksman (the manager), Tom McColm, Harry Stevenson, John Duckworth, Jack Barrett, Terry Tighe, Dick Briggs and Michael Kneafsey.

A lady of my acquaintance boarded a Corporation bus in the mid-1950s and overheard a conversation which concerned a man who was a Stanley full-back. It appears that this man had been *'playing away'* with another man's wife. This man found out about it and shot the full-back. One of the passengers in the conversation remarked at this point *"Aye, that bullet were th'only thing he ever bloody stopped"*.

✕✕✕

This photograph of the Sacred Heart *'scholars'* participating in a procession along Blackburn Road was taken about 1910, when gentlemen wore top hats.

EARLY CATHOLIC EFFORTS IN ACCRINGTON

Leo Warren

In his return made in 1767 to the Anglican Bishop of Chester, the Licensed Curate of Altham and Accrington gave details of the 86 Catholics or *'Papists'* living within his chapelry. Of these, nine lived at Dunkenhalgh where for ten years Mr. James Heatley had acted as Agent for Lady Stourton who, in 1712 as the young Catherine Walmesley, had married Lord Petre.

Throughout the eighteenth century the family maintained at Dunkenhalgh a Jesuit priest as chaplain. In practice he also served the needs of the local Catholics. In 1767, Fr. Andrew Thorpe S.J. was in residence and his flock numbered some 130 souls if the Catholics in Harwood, Rishton and Church Kirk are included. A recent convert was Mr. James Lomax of Clayton Hall.

When, in 1818, Dunkenhalgh Chapel was closed it was James Lomax's son who took the lead in establishing the new Catholic Church at St. Mary's Enfield. It was opened on 11th July 1819. The first resident priest was Fr. Charles Brooke S.J. who as a boy had studied at the Jesuit college in Liège, and had taken part in the flight from Liège to Stonyhurst in 1794 at the time of the French Revolution.

The new chapel in Burnley Road beyond the canal bridge was quite substantial: it accommodated some 400 people and the congregation was expanding all the time. The priest who was to make the greatest impact was Fr. John Leadbetter S.J. He arrived at Enfield in 1833 and would be there for forty years. He was popular and energetic. A keen musician, under him the choir and brass band flourished. He established in 1837 a Sunday school using money left in memory of Adela Petre. In that year 170 children, 80 boys and 90 girls, were attending catechism at 2.30 pm on Sundays. He also laid out the first burial ground.

In 1851 the Religious Census recorded that on Census Sunday 520 attended the 10.30 Mass including the 200 children who returned in the afternoon for Sunday School. These figures give us a picture of the Catholic Congregation when St. Mary's was still the only Catholic Chapel in the whole Accrington area. This was soon to change.

It had been announced the previous November that *'the want of accommodation in the Chapel and School of St. Mary's Enfield for the numerous and increasing Catholic population, together with the very inconvenient distance that great numbers are subject to'* made it necessary to build a new substantial school and schoolhouse. Mr. Henry Petre of Dunkenhalgh gave an acre of land, part of Riding Barn Farm, in Hyndburn Road, between Accrington and Church. (Opposite where, in later years, Hyndburn Park School was built)

The new school building was to be in the Gothic style from designs presented by Joseph Hansom, the architect of the recently completed Catholic Chapel in Clitheroe and of St. Walburge's in Preston, then being built, but famous also for designing the *'Hansom cab'*. Mr. Petre had promised to lay the first stone on the 2nd October 1851, but in the event was not able to be present, though he did donate a further £500 and so enabled Fr. Leadbetter, *'the originator and indefatigable promoter of the work'* to finish the undertaking. Despite Mr. Petre's generosity, more funds were needed to meet the cost of the building. Besides collections and Charity Sermons, other efforts included a superbly-wrought quilt, the workmanship and charitable contribution of Miss Wilkinson, the school mistress. It was put up for lottery and realised £20.

It was reported on the 30th October 1852 in the Preston Guardian that *'notwithstanding the extremely liberal gift that accompanied the grant of land, together with other generous offerings, the School is still in debt. (It cost £1,700) It is to be hoped that the untiring zeal of the reverend promoter of the meritorious work (Fr. Leadbetter) will on the 4th and 7th of next month witness a corresponding activity on the part of the public, especially from those who so frequently and so warmly advocate the course of moral and intellectual improvement of their neighbours. Independently of the motive of charity, the building deserves a visit on account of its being so ingeniously constructed, and its various apartments so judiciously arranged that it may be justly looked upon as a model Chapel for Sundays and a model School for weekdays'.* Readers were confidently assured that the new school was within two minutes walk from the stations at Accrington and Church where the trains stopped every second hour.

On Thursday 4th November 1852 the school was opened as St. Oswald's with the celebration of Mass and on the following Sunday there were special services and collections.

Sadly, within the month, Mr. Henry Petre died and was buried in Enfield Chapel. It was recorded that *'the Poor of Enfield have lost a kind and benevolent friend'.* Three years later his youngest son Oswald Petre died from fever contracted in the Crimean War. He too was buried in Enfield Chapel. Soon there was further bad news. Among the first priests to serve at St. Oswald's was Fr. Jerrard Strickland. Appointed in 1854, he then volunteered his services as chaplain in the Crimean War. He died there in April 1856 of camp fever caught as he attended French soldiers. The celebrations marking the end of that war in 1856 began the tradition of the annual Catholic Procession.

The congregation at St. Oswald's continued to expand rapidly and soon a bigger and separate church was planned. Its foundation stone was laid in 1867, just one hundred years after that Return had been sent to the Bishop of Chester. Four hundred children from St. Oswald's walked in procession via Church to the new site in Blackburn Road for the ceremony. The thirty priests present included Fr. Leadbetter, still at Enfield, and Fr. Alfred Weld, the Jesuit Provincial. He announced that the new church would be dedicated to the Sacred Heart, and as such, despite many difficulties, was opened in August 1869. St. Oswald's School continued in Hyndburn Road and its name survived when it moved to more spacious premises in Willow Lane in 1872. This was to be the first of the school's many moves. Of Hansom's original building in Hyndburn Road, only the two attractive stone cottages still survive, reminders of Fr. Leadbetter's great enterprise in Accrington. Think of these Christian pioneers to Accrington as you pass by *'Rose Cottage'* and *'Ivy Cottage'.*

THE ODD FELLOWS OF ACCRINGTON

Pauline M. Hutchinson

The Manchester Unity of Odd Fellows evolved in the year 1810 from the Union or London Order. The principal benefit in the early days was 'travelling relief' providing bed and board on a daily basis to members travelling in search of employment. In 1813 the Manchester Lodges formed an Independent Order, so named, because they were independent of the original Union. A year later the Order formed a Committee which, after 1821, met annually to pass general laws for better management of the Order.

The early benefits were all regarded as 'gifts' as they were in the nature of benevolent grants in sickness, the travelling benefit, or on the death of a member or his wife. Later, members paid weekly to make provision against sickness, old age and death.

The Odd Fellows first appeared in Accrington in 1825 when the Rose on the Hill Lodge was formed in Clayton le Moors, although there were probably unregistered meetings before that. Meetings were held in the Commercial Hotel, St. James School and an Odd Fellows Hall which is now the Come and Welcome Club.

Over the years, nine lodges developed in Accrington, Huncoat, Oswaldtwistle, Rishton and Great Harwood and in these early days the meetings were usually in public houses. The Lily of the Valley Lodge of Accrington originally met in the Odd Fellows Home (a beerhouse on the corner of Little Blackburn Road and Bank Street (now William Hill's Bookmakers) and later in the Commercial Hotel which is now the Regency. The Highbrake Lodge of Huncoat met at the White Lion; Foxhill Dale Lodge of Church met at the Stag Hotel;. Patience Lodge of Great Harwood met at the Dog and Otter and Hopeful Lodge in Oswaldtwistle met at the Tinker and Budget. Prosperity Lodge, however never met in a public house but in rooms over Burnley Building Society in Blackburn Road, Accrington and Pleasant Valley Lodge met in the Co-operative Rooms at Rishton.

The Odd Fellows had many investments in property and granted mortgages to members. The Odd Fellows Terrace dated 1895 in Cliff Street, Rishton must have been owned by the Society at some time. There was an Odd Fellows Court in Moore Street, Accrington but this has disappeared with the construction of the inner relief road, Eastgate. Club Street in Great Harwood (later renamed Ward Street) was built in 1854 at a time when there were no mortgages. Instead, people formed clubs to enable them to buy their own houses. One of these clubs was the Odd Fellows.

Another property with possible connections with the Society is the Odd Fellows Arms on Whalley Road, Clayton le Moors. This row, originally known as Canal Row, Enfield Street, was built in 1815 as handloom weavers' cottages with a half yearly ground rent of £1. 3s. 3d. per cottage. Over the years, it was listed as a beerhouse under different people's names. In the Street Directory for 1872 it was owned by a Mr. Robert Sharples and according to the census, Robert Sharples also had another job and was married to Mary Sharples. By 1876 it is listed in the name of Mrs. Mary Sharples, so presumably Robert had died and his wife had taken over. In the 1878 Directory the name of the beerhouse is changed to the Odd Fellows Arms but still linked with the name of Mary Sharples. Also the road name changed when Clayton le Moors was formed from the two hamlets of Enfield and Oakenshaw. It is assumed from this information that either Robert Sharples was an Odd Fellow and when he died Mary named the beerhouse after him, or the Odd Fellows loaned her money to carry on the business on her own. For years the sign outside the pub was just a plain red board with the words *'Oddfellows'* but when the pub was refurbished ten years ago, the board was replaced with the Coat of Arms and three links of the Manchester Unity of Odd Fellows. It is not thought that this building was ever used for a meeting of an Odd Fellows' Lodge.

In the past, the Manchester Unity of Odd Fellows were really the forerunners of the National Health Service providing financial assistance in sickness and help with dental and optical costs. The Orphan Gift Fund has provided a good education to orphans of members and individual lodges have donated many sums of money to charities. This work is still going on but unfortunately the membership is dwindling. So much so that the nine lodges of Accrington have now amalgamated into just two lodges - *'Rose on the Hill Lodge'* and *'Prosperity Lodge'* which meet jointly in the Community Room at Banbury Close, Accrington.

WE ARE WELL ENDOWED

In 1899, the Charity Commissioners visited Accrington to enquire into and place on record the various endowments which had been made for the benefit of Accrington's needy. They discovered there were many separate endowments, and listed them

1. *The National School*. At a meeting in 1816, it was resolved by, amongst others, Rev. Hopwood of St. James' Church and members of the Peel and Hargreaves families, as well as the inhabitants who attended, that a school for the town's poor should be erected. A 'subscription' (collection) was started to buy land, build and support a school. William Dutton sold, for £75, a plot of land called 'Chapel Holme', 24 yards by 25 yards, for the school house. The education provided was to be on the 'national system'. (Here we see why Dutton Street and Holme Street are so called)

In 1823, Betty Rostron left £10 to the school's trustees. In 1824, Jonathan Peel gave £1,000, and in 1854 Robert Hargreaves left it £200. That same amount was given in 1863 by Mrs. Helen Stansfield 'to be applied for the benefit of the organist and choir'.

The Commissioners learned that, in 1845, a site had been bought in Peel Street for a school for the infants of St. James' Church (This is why Infant Street is so called). The school had cost £3,500 to build. In 1895, a new school had been erected between Cannon Street and Paradise Street. The old site and house had been sold and the monies put towards the fund. Wise investments had been made, even though Betty Rostron's money had been used up by 1863. By 1899, 130 children attended the school.

2. *Mrs. Cunliffe's Charity*. Mrs. Catherine Cunliffe died in 1756, but forty years previously she had given £5 to purchase Bibles. There had also been annual payments into the fund by its trustees, the Duckworth family, but by 1816 these had stopped. The residents complained, resulting in Lawrence Duckworth paying £7 in for 14 years arrears. The family estate had passed to Nicholas Worsley of the Laund, including the need to pay an annual sum for the provision, by the curate, of Bibles and Prayer Books for the poor in Old and New Accrington.

The Commissioners found 'the principal sum of £10 was lost many years ago. Worsley does not appear to have attended to the recommendation of the 1826 Commissioners, as nothing has been heard of it since'.

3. *Darwen's Charity*. In 1899, 18 loaves costing 3d were distributed on the first Sunday

of the month to the poor at Church Kirk Church. The income came from the rents of 8 cottages on Church Kirk Lane. The original donation was of £60, and this *'now brings in £3 per annum.'* (1899)

4. *Cross Street*, or *Adam Dugdale's Charity*. In 1840, certain Accrington cottages were conveyed to the vicar of St. James' Church, his churchwardens and the Overseers of the Poor of Old and New Accrington. Adam Dugdale bequeathed £100 towards the £230 needed to buy the cottages, the rest coming from various inhabitants. In 1898, the cottages were sold for £2,930. They were on land in Oak Street and Cannon Street, and included 'The Borough Arms'. When invested, this was 'now bringing in £79 19s 4d per annum'.

The charity's managers paid out in March and December, usually giving a florin to each person. In December 1898, 311 persons received a total of £31 1s 0d.

5. *Accrington Cotton Famine Relief Fund*. In 1862, a relief fund was established in the town for alleviating the distress amongst operatives in the cotton trade. (The 'Cotton Famine' had just started, the result of Lancashire mills not receiving American cotton due to the Civil War there) A larger amount was collected than was needed, and in 1871 (?) £420 was put into an account for public relief, this sum being applied for the purchase of land, 8 houses and some buildings. The fund paid out to 24 persons between August and October 1898, amounts ranging from 5 shillings to £1 2s 6d, a total of £15 10s 0d. The previous year £26 16s 8d had been distributed.

6. *Wilson's Charity*. In 1850, Benjamin Wilson of Baxenden bequeathed £800 in trust for the organist at St. James' Church, to the churchwardens there, and to the schoolmaster at Baxenden School. In 1899, £22 was split five ways and applied according to his will.

7. *Hall's Charity*. Charles Hall of Gothic House, in his will of 1882, left £200 to the vicar and churchwardens of St. James' Church, directing that it should be invested in railway stocks, the income to pay for cassocks and surplices for the choir - 'but not for the washing, cleaning or getting-up of them'. In 1899, the dividend brought in £5 8s 8d per year.

8. *Stansfield's Bequest*. Dr. Edgar Stansfield left £1,000 to St. James' Church in his 1872 will. The churchwardens put some towards the rebuilding, and loaned some to the Corporation at 2%.

9. *Hopwood's Charity*. Miss Elizabeth Hopwood of Bristol, in her will of 1879 provided £500 for the benefit of St. James' Sunday School, and another £500 (both sums to be invested) for the poor of Accrington, to be distributed after divine service on Christmas Day. Widows were to be given preference. (I suspect that she was the daughter of Rev. John Hopwood, the church's vicar, who was the town's only magistrate in the early years of the 19th century)

10. *Robert Holt's Charity*. Robert Holt (1879) bequeathed £200 to the wardens of Christ Church, the interest to be applied to 'beautifying the interior of the Church'. In 1899 there was £15 in hand, the original sum now bringing £5 11s 0d yearly.

11. *Hargreaves' Charity*. Benjamin Hargreaves died in 1880, leaving £300 to be invested by the vicar of St. John's Church, the dividends to be applied to church repairs. In 1899 this brought in £6 per year.

12. *New Accrington Wesleyan Chapel*. The church had been built in 1864 on a piece of land measuring 2,383 square yards. In 1874 and 1877, the trustees acquired some land, shops and houses in Spring Gardens and Abbey Street. Subsequently the Corporation bought a house and some land from them for £750. This, invested at 4%, was applied to the chapel's purpose.

13. *Jubilee Poor Fund*. In 1897, to commemorate Victoria's sixty years on the throne,

William Horrock Rawson and James Herbert Rawson gave £1,000 to start The Jubilee Poor Fund, for the benefit of poor and deserving persons in the Borough. The Rawsons were connected with Union Street Methodists and the fund was to be administered by a local Methodist.

14. *Duxbury Charities*. Joseph Duxbury died in 1896, leaving £3,000 for 'poor and necessitous persons not under the age of 65 years as were natives and residents (of Accrington)', also £500 towards a technical school, £500 for a high-grade school, £500 towards the making of Oak Hill Park, £500 for establishing public baths and £300 towards a cottage hospital. Truly, his generousity knew no bounds.

15. *Mercer's Charity*. Robert Clayton Mercer of Oakenshaw House died in 1882, directing his executors to invest a sum sufficient to raise £25 per annum to be distributed annually in coal, clothing or food, to the poor of Clayton. The sum needed (1899) for this was £833 6s 8d. Distribution took place at Christmas in the form of about 80 5-shilling tickets.

16. *Walmesley's Charities*. Benjamin Walmesley died in 1853, leaving £100 for the churchwardens of Ossie to invest so that the proceeds would provide bread. Every alternate Sunday, 8 poor women were supplied with a 2-pounds loaf, costing 3d. They also got an extra loaf or cake at Christmas. He also left £100 to supplement the vicar's stipend. At some time later, Robert Walmesley gave £100 towards the stipend, and in 1886, George Walmesley, who lived at the Paddock, gave a piece of land, the rent of which (£9 in 1899) went to the vicar. This land was rented by a butcher, presumably for keeping cattle and sheep on before...... George died in 1891, leaving £250 to Immanuel Church to be used towards the cost of the Sunday and Day Schools. He also left £250 to benefit the vicar's stipend, as well as £3,000 to be used by the vicars of Immanuel, the Wesleyan Chapel, Mount Pleasant and the Roman Catholic Church, Moscow Mill Street, for distribution to the 'necessitous residents within the limits of Oswaldtwistle' who had lived there for five years and were 60 years old or more. This committee was to meet under Walmesley's daughter and distribute quarterly. Poverty and good character were the main qualifications, also (1899) an aggregate income earned by the household of less than one shilling a week. The number relieved varied form 50 to 86. Relief was given in groceries and clothing to the value of five shillings.

That was the situation in 1899. I would dearly like to be able to give a full picture now, almost a century on. I can fill in some pieces of the jig-saw:-

In 1912, Church and Ossie Urban District Councils arranged a collection which raised £262 19s 7d, most of which was invested in shares in the British Cotton Growers Association, the income being applied to needy persons in those townships. Present-day councillors are today's trustees of the £152,779 held. (1994)

In 1938, the *Accrington Queen's District Nursing Association* was founded to benefit the sick of Accrington, Clayton and Altham. In 1951 it became the *Accrington District Sick Poor Fund*.

In 1983, the *Dugdale (Cross Street) Charity* and the *Duxbury Charities* were joined together to become the *Accrington Relief in Need Charity*. It is active today, the trustees being council nominated people administering the capital of £24,783. (1994)

In 1983, similarly, the *Robert Clayton Mercer Charity* joined with the *T. W. Bracewell Charity* to become the *Clayton-le-Moors Relief in Need Charity*.

108

AN AMERICAN IN ACCRINGTON

In 1886, Dr. Wayland, an American Baptist minister, visited Accrington and stayed with Rev. Charles Williams. His impressions were printed in an American Baptist magazine, and re-printed in the first edition of the *'Accrington Observer'* in 1887:-

"Accrington is a town of about 32,000 inhabitants, lying in the coal region; its industries are mainly coal mines, cotton mills and iron works. Like most of the manufacturing towns it is strongly Liberal and Nonconformist. The Mayor is a Methodist. The Cannon-street Baptist Chapel is quite the first church edifice in the town, not excepting the Parish Church. But the hearing properties are not proportioned to its beauty or its expense. Owing to the cruciform shape or to the abundance of pillars, it is very hard to hear in. The congregation is large, intelligent and enterprising. Before the sermon in the morning I carried out a purpose which had been in my head for years. In 1863, when I was serving in the United States in the South, I read that people in Lancashire (the plain, labouring people, not the millionaires), when the rich millionaires were urging the Government to unite with France in breaking the blockade, and thus put an end to the cotton famine, said: suffering as we are from shortness of work and shortness of bread, we will hold a bit longer; we and our children will bear the famine, rather than that you shall help to break up the Republic which is the hope of free government, rather than that you shall injure our brothers the Americans. My heart flowed out in tears; I could have kissed the ground on which those men stood. And I have always wanted to thank the people of Lancashire. And so, on that day, I was permitted, standing in a pulpit in Lancashire, to express the gratitude which I and America owe them".

Dr. Wayland was entertained by Mr. G. W. Macalpine, with whom he went to visit Willow Street School. "The Master - Mr. A. Langham - is an interesting progressive man. I was interested in hearing him say, as the result of his experience, that two-thirds of the all too scanty time which the children spent in school is wasted in the effort to teach them the false, misleading, puzzle-headed lie which we call spelling. The teachers have to make a perpetual struggle in order to root out from the minds of the children the Lancashire dialect, which is almost another tongue. A stranger, hearing two working-men converse in the street, would scarcely understand a word.

We then went into the buildings of the Liberal Club. Here, hanging up over the mantle, neatly framed, is the telegram which came to the club on election evening, giving the figure at Midlothian, and the majority for Mr. Gladstone. This was framed and presented by a working-man. No doubt the incident was representative. Very many among the leaders of the party have left Mr. Gladstone; but no one can mingle with the plain people, the rank and file, and especially with the Nonconformists, without realising that to them Mr. Gladstone is first, and there is no second…. We then went into a spinning and weaving mill carried on by Mr. Haworth. I wanted to see the working-people at their work, and to, learn a bit about their condition. I was satisfied with all I saw. The air was free from dust and flakes of cotton; the men and women and children seemed in good health, and were earning fair wages. One man who occupied a position of considerable responsibility, and who works over hours, was getting £2 13s 0d a week; but this was rather extraordinary; others were getting 25s to 30s. The grown girls get 5s 7½d a week for each loom, and run three or four looms, paying two small girls half-a-crown each for helping. The girls and boys of 10 to 13 work only half time, i.e. only five hours. The large boys get 17s to 18s".

Dr. Weyland next visited the Altham Collieries of which he says, "I determined to go to the bottom of the matter, so I went down 285 yards. I was not afraid that the bottom would drop out, but that the top would drop in. It was 12 o'clock; the boys of 12 to 13 were quitting work, their half time being up; their faces were black, but they seemed cheerful and happy; they would go to school in the afternoon; for half time they got half-a-crown per week. The men get rather better wages than in the mill, some getting £2 per week. One man, when work was better than now, saved £100 in a year. The shafts seemed well ventilated by the great fan. I was amazed and struck all of a heap to learn that the 'Davy Safety Lamp' is no longer of any use, and that it ought to be prohibited in the mines. It was adapted to the former state of things, but is unsuited to the currents of air caused by the great fan, and is now a source of danger.

The Government inspection of the mills and mines is very strict; there is no nonsense about it; if the precautions for health and safety are not observed, if the boys work overtime, or if they are employed when they have not attended school properly, the owner is fined. It would not be possible to see, as one may see all over New Jersey and Pennsylvania, young children working ten and twelve and thirteen hours. The working man's money goes further than it does in America; he gets a four-roomed house, well built, for 4s a week, he pays 10s a ton for his coal, delivered; his clothing is cheaper; his gas is much cheaper. I speak simply of what I have seen; not of places that I have not seen; in those the conditions may all be, very likely are, much worse. But what I saw of the working people of Lancashire was, as a whole, encouraging and gratifying".

CHARITY BEGINS AT THE TOWN HALL

The winter of 1890/1 was bleak. A severe, lengthy frost threw all outdoor workers out of employment. Dire distress overwhelmed very many families. Seeing this, the Mayor, Thomas Whittaker, called the Town Clerk and the Chief Constable to his office on 10th January 1891 and told them to get a free soup kitchen started. By 8 pm that day, one had been set up in the Town Hall and 180 people given soup and bread. It was realised that thinking had to be on a bigger scale, and so kitchens were also established in Wesley School, in Mr. Southworth's shop in Warner Street and in a room over the Fire Station behind the Market Hall. This last one was for children only. For 14 days, an average of 400 meals were given out in that room to 133 little ones.

In the audited report some months afterwards, the generosity of many individuals and groups was acknowledged: Hartley Goddard, a butcher in Abbey Street, had given 200 lbs of potted meat and 100 loaves; Amos Ashworth, chemist in Blackburn Road, gave 53 lbs of tea; the Co-op provided 25 cowheads, a sheep and some coal; The Gas & Water Company gave the Mayor tickets for free coke for every needy person in the borough; the Conservatives loaned a portable boiler.

The Mayor publicly thanked the many people who had given £135 17s 10d, and he chucked in £11 8s 8d to add to it, which came to the £147 6s 6d spent in the 17-day exercise. His staff, mostly the Borough Police, had seen babies who hadn't eaten for a whole day, children weeping with the pain of hunger, and men enduring hunger so that their children could eat. To help mitigate the distress, the soup diet was varied to allow for

The Town Hall about 100 years ago. Note the doorway on the left hand side - it isn't there today.

Accrington.

The Wrench Series. No. 6058.

The Town Hall.

helpings of potato pie, bread, tea and potted meat, all served up by the Fire Brigade, Police and willing helpers. The Town Hall Relief Fund gave out 95 pairs of clogs, 3,315 lbs of meat, 3,358 gallons of soup and 4,294 loaves. In all, 5,493 meals were given to starving children. Private Christian charity was acknowledged too. For instance, Mr. Dunstan, a butcher in Blackburn Road, gave soup out from his shop.

I fancy that, as happened at a Manchester Police Soup Kitchen, prayers would accompany the feeding. A grace was probably sung:-

> "Be present at our table, Lord
> Be here and everywhere adored.
> Thy children bless and grant that we
> May feast in Paradise with Thee."

✳✳✳✳✳✳

The *'Accrington Observer'* on 1st January 1887 told of a tea party - referred to as a Christmas Tea Meeting - being held in Union Street Methodist School in 1830. 36 people were present - the writer, R. Bradley, names them, even mentioning that amongst them were *'Ann Holden of George's and Ann Holden of John's'*. He details the individual cost of the 20 lbs of flour, the quarter pound of green tea and the half pound of black tea, the 4 lbs of sugar, 6 lbs of butter, the candles and the cream, all of which cost seventeen shillings, seven pence ha'penny.

111

ACCRINGTON'S TRAMCARS.

Robert W. Rush.

Few people today will remember the bright red and cream electric trams which trundled around Accrington for almost twenty five years from August 1907 until January 1932. They operated along the four main roads out of the town; to Church and Oswaldtwistle (Black Dog); to the canal bridge at Clayton; to Baxenden station; and up Burnley Road to the cemetery gates. The Burnley Road route was always the Cinderella of the system; it never paid its way, but had it been extended, as was proposed, to Huncoat village, it might have been a different story. Only when there were football or cricket matches did the route carry any great amount of traffic.

Nominally all four routes began in Peel Street, but in practice the Oswaldtwistle and Burnley Road lines were operated as a through route, and at weekends the Clayton cars ran through to Church. Owing to the low railway bridge at Church station, only single deck cars could work to Oswaldtwistle. From 1909 onwards the Baxenden route was extended to Rawtenstall - this having to wait for the expiry of the lease of the Rawtenstall steam tramways before the line could be electrified. There was also an end-on junction at Church with the Blackburn Corporation tramways, but it was not until 1917 that the two authorities came to an agreement for running a through service. Though nominally terminating at the Market Place, the Clayton and Rawtenstall cars actually worked along Blackburn Road to the bottom of Eagle Street, reversing on a crossover there, and passengers were allowed to travel this extra distance without charge. The fleet was quite a considerable one, numbering thirty eight cars, of which thirteen were single deck. Most of them were four-wheeled, but from 1914 onwards five single-deck and four double-deck, enclosed cars with eight wheels were purchased; these operated mostly at weekends, but some were also used at peak periods.

Fares were ridiculously low compared with the present day. One could travel to Oswaldtwistle, Clayton, or Baxenden for three old pennies, and through to Blackburn for five pence. There were also return fares at about one and a half times the single fare, and early morning and evening workmen's fares for around half the normal fee. In addition there were special reduced fares for schoolchildren and blind persons. Incidentally, a complete driver's uniform - cap, jacket, trousers and overcoat - cost £2 17s 6d.

A tram's capacity for shifting passengers was phenomenal. Standing was allowed only on the lower deck, but there was no limit, as many as could find room were allowed, which did not make the collecting of fares any easier. I do not know the figures for Accrington, but the official record for a Blackburn eight-wheeled tram (72 seats) was 198 passengers on a football special. The conductor gave up to collecting the fares! Trams were also the safest form of public transport, with their two (or sometimes three) independent braking systems they could literally stop on a sixpence in emergency. Accrington had the enviable reputation of never killing a passenger (though there were several minor injuries due to mishaps) and only three tramway employees lost their lives, two through serious collisions, and one who fell from a cleaning gantry in the depot.

Driver Murdock was killed in an accident in thick fog at Rising Bridge. Driving car No. 22, he collided head on with a Ribble bus, which was travelling much too fast under the conditions. The bus driver was charged with manslaughter, but was acquitted on appeal. Murdock, who was well over six feet in height, was a popular employee with both passengers and staff.

Trams were very useful in thick fogs. They would always get you to your destination and they used to accumulate a long tail of motor and horse vehicles tagging on behind, in the knowledge that wherever a tram could go, others could follow, with no danger of running off the road. An amusing episode in thick fog was when a Rawtenstall car on the through service got completely lost, and instead of turning back at Eagle Street, went through to Church. When the driver finally realised he was way off his route, he was obliged to go on to Blackburn Corporation tracks to reverse.

There were one or two characters who worked on the trams. One driver sported a long flowing white beard, which on the open ended cars often draped itself over the dashplate. How he managed to operate the control handles without getting his beard tangled in them is anybody's guess. For some unknown reason he was known as the *'Mayor of Laneside'*. A diminutive conductor who worked for many years could easily be mistaken for one of Brooke Bond's chimps, so simian was his appearance. I remember many years later, when he was conducting on the buses, we were at a stop, with everything quiet, when my elder daughter, then aged five, suddenly piped up *"Mum, doesn't that man look like a monkey?"* The bus exploded in laughter, and my wife and I wished we could dive under the seats. Luckily the conductor joined in the laughter, saying he was used to it, and it didn't worry him in the least. A third character was a Dutch refugee who had come to England in 1914 and settled in Accrington. He had an unpronounceable Dutch name, and the staff soon started calling him *'The Hollander'*, so he changed his name by deed poll to *'Holland'*.

I remember, as a boy, in bed at night (if I wasn't fast asleep) hearing the last car coming down Burnley Road about 11 p.m. I could hear it start from the terminus, with the double bang as it passed over the rail joints, and the clatter as it went over the points of the four

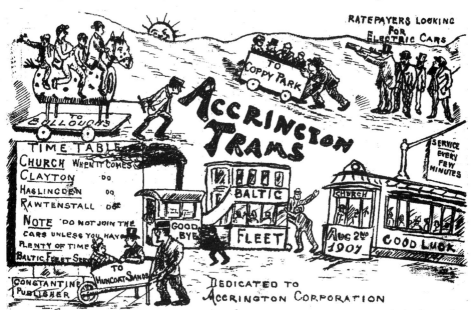

Local photographer Constantine produced this postcard to commemorate the changeover from steam to electrically powered trams on 15th April 1907.

113

passing loops, right down to the bottom of Burnley Road. The driver of that last car used to put on speed, far in excess of the statutory 12 m.p.h., and in the quietness of those nights, the car's progress was unmistakeable.

In the mid-1920s tramcars became extremely unpopular - a situation instigated by the fledgling bus industry - and all sorts of allegations were made against them; they were slow, noisy, uncomfortable, impeded other traffic, hogged the middle of the road, and so on. This theme was taken up by the media, and gradually the various tramway operators were convinced, scrapped their fleets, and replaced them by buses. Most disappeared between 1928 and 1935, leaving only a handful of cities and large towns, such as Glasgow, Liverpool, Manchester, London, etc. still maintaining their trams. Blackburn hung on until 1949, and only Blackpool and the Isle of Man refused to bow to the outcry. All the rest had gone by 1963. As far as Accrington goes, the rot set in in 1930, when Rawtenstall decided to scrap its system; from then onwards Accrington gradually followed suit. At the end of 1931 only the Burnley Road route remained, awaiting the delivery of four new buses. When these appeared, the last tram ran down Burnley Road on January 6th 1932. The four double-deck eight-wheeled cars were sold to Southend, and continued to work there until 1942; the five similar single-deckers went to Llandudno, and survived until 1956. Several of the four-wheeled car bodies became henhouses, sports pavilions, and garden sheds, scattered around the district, but all had disappeared by the end of the war. The Accrington trams were always well maintained and well cleaned; until late 1931, it was very rare to see one which was not spick and span.

Riley's swing bridge, between Church and Clayton, is almost half-way by canal from Liverpool and Leeds. In the distance is Whin Isle farm and Enfield House.

ACCRINGTON'S CANAL CONNECTION

Mike Clarke

As the Leeds and Liverpool Canal winds its tortuous way through East Lancashire, it seems to carefully avoid Accrington. In fact, the town was the largest hereabouts not be served by the canal. This was never the intention. When the canal's route through East Lancashire was decided in 1793, it was planned to continue up the valley of the Hyndburn, crossing it at a point close to the old Grammar School on Blackburn Road. The proposed Haslingden Canal was to join it here, creating a water link with Bury and Manchester. Had this happened, there would have been a wharf near the junction where goods to and from the town could have been handled.

Instead, the route was altered. The Peel family asked the canal company to avoid crossing the Hyndburn above their printing works at Peel Bank. At that time it was one of the largest factories in the world and used the clear waters of the Hyndburn (How things changed later!) for washing the cloth during the printing process. Building the embankment necessary for the canal to cross the Hyndburn would have interrupted this supply and caused production problems. A short branch along the original line did serve the factory, but the main line was built downstream, rejoining the original line at a right angle junction at Church. Much of the land for the canal deviation had to be purchased from the Petre family of Dunkenhalgh. Although they were quite happy for the canal to be built, they requested that the towpath was made on the side of the canal away from their house and lands. They hoped that this would prevent poachers from gaining easy access to their estate!

Accrington's lack of a canal was seen as a major disadvantage, and a branch canal was proposed on two occasions, in 1875 and 1882. The small branch built for the Peels would have been extended along the northern side of the Hyndburn, ending in a circular canal just below the railway viaduct. Besides providing condensing water for mill steam engines, the branch would have been used to bring coal to the gasworks and grain to the corn mill. A rather less savoury cargo would have been refuse and nightsoil. After collection from the bin 'oyls and closets in the back entries of local terraced houses, it would have been delivered by boat to West Lancashire for spreading on farm fields as manure. The sewage works at Church certainly provided such cargoes into the 1940s. Unfortunately, the branch would have been expensive to build, unlikely to pay for itself and was never built.

Up until the early 1960s, when carrying by canal ceased, Accrington had to rely upon the wharves at Enfield and Church for its canal service. The former, opened in 1801, was built near to the junction of two turnpike roads which enabled goods to be carried to and from Bury and Clitheroe besides serving Accrington. The warehouses, which still stand, are now used by small businesses and by the Sea Cadets. Several factories were served by the canal at Enfield; of particular note are Royal Mill, the last to be built in Clayton, which opened in 1912, and Enfield Corn Mill, used for many years by Joseph Appleby, who had his own fleet of boats carrying grain on the canal. This mill was subsequently occupied by the East Lancashire Soap Company who used the canal for shipping their famous floating soap. Presumably, it must have been carried by boat! The history of the canal at Church is, perhaps, more interesting. The turnpike from Blackburn to Accrington was opened after the canal and the canal embankment across Tinker Brook was enlarged to carry the road as well. The first canalside warehouse was opened in 1836, a few years afterwards. This was

115

built by the Hargreaves brothers of Broad Oak. A proper wharf was erected seven years later, the canal company draining the canal for just twenty four hours to allow the foundations to be built. The canal company later took over the warehouse, enlarging and improving the facilities in 1890. They also built a wharf at the end of Bradley Street which opened in 1891. Built on the site of the Church Lane Chemical Works, it was used for the storage of timber and machinery. Because they had little space at their factory, Howard and Bullough's were one of the main users of this wharf. The canal company would then deliver their export textile machinery right to the ship's side in the docks at Liverpool, Birkenhead or even Hull. Thomas Crawshaw, a local coal merchant, also provided a collection and delivery service from the wharf. He cannot have been too reliable as the canal company took over this part of his business in 1901, paying £700 for his stable, horses and lurries. The canal company had further problems at Church in that year as J. W. Varley, their agent there, was dismissed because of irregularities in his accounts. Things had improved by 1913 when an electric crane was installed to help with loading and unloading.

Four years later, the routine operation of the canal was upset once again. To supply the munitions industry, Lance Blythe had set up the Coteholme and Kirk Chemical Companies which made picric acid and high explosives. On the 27th April 1917 a fire started at the works. James Hardacre, a policeman at Church, was killed while attempting to ensure that everyone had left the site. He was awarded the King's Police Medal posthumously. There was large scale damage throughout Church. The houses in Bradley Street and Canal Street bore the brunt of the explosion, while Church Kirk was closed until the following August. The canal also suffered as four boats, towed by a tug, were passing at the time. The explosion blew the tarpaulin covers off the cargoes and the boatmen must have been shocked. The wharf, which was directly opposite the factory, was also damaged, the company reporting:

The electric and steam derrick cranes were slightly damaged, cases of the machinery belonging to Messrs. Howard and Bullough protected by the waterproof cover were set on fire, the electric switch house and stabling consisting of 19 stalls with lofts over them, 3 loose boxes, cart shed and harness room were more or less demolished. The horses were got out uninjured...Owing to war conditions only nine horses are now employed whereas in normal conditions the stabling is fully occupied.

There was also an 8-horse stable, but this only had its roof blown off and it was quickly repaired. Due to wartime restrictions, little about the explosion was made public. The wharf was rebuilt and continued in operation for many years. New warehouses were erected in the 1950s and '60s, with road transport using them after carrying on the canal finished. The wharf ceased being used in 1985 when a fire burnt out one of the new warehouses.

(Leeds and Liverpool Canal)

The LANCASHIRE CANAL TRANSPORT Co LTD

General Carriers & Storage Contractors

USE THE CANAL

THE IRON ROAD

In 1931, there was a liaison between the Corporation and the management at *'Bullough's'* which promised much, in particular much-needed employment at the Globe Works. A Major Small had recently patented a cast-iron block to replace the expensive granite setts then in use for road surfaces. Experimental roads of these blocks had been laid down in different parts of the country, and a Corporation delegation had visited West Ham to view one. With County Council permission, it was agreed that the local firm would manufacture sufficient to be laid, in a fifteen-feet wide stretch between Plantation Street and Black Abbey Street, on a concrete foundation. The blocks were shaped as an equilateral triangle, $11^1/_2$ inches long and weighed $10^1/_2$ lbs each (that's five bags of sugar).

It was laid, but the experiment appears not to have had the desired results. I was told by my father that a horse-drawn lorry had skidded on the surface and killed a young girl, but I suspect that this was folk-lore not founded on fact. Whatever the reason, the blocks were taken up and replaced by more a conventional surface about 1938.

One of Accrington's Leyland Lion single deck buses, no. 42, purchased around 1927, makes its way to Baxenden over the 'Iron Road'.

THE BRICKWORKS RAILWAY.

Robert W. Rush.

About half way along the railway line between Accrington and Huncoat stations, the train comes out of a cutting and under a bridge. On the left is the Accrington cricket ground, while on the right is the municipal cemetery. At this point, adjoining the cricket ground, there used to be a signal box controlling a loop line from which branched out four sidings. These, and the signal box, were officially known as *'Brick Sidings'*. Where these stood for over seventy years there is now only a space with nothing but rank grass upon it. A century ago, a single railway line led from these sidings, to the north behind the Cricket Club pavilion. In some three or four hundred yards it crossed over a public footpath by a primitive bridge, and divided into two. The left hand fork from this junction turned north-westerly and, running dead straight for three quarters of a mile, entered the yard of the Nori Brickworks. The right hand fork turned north-easterly on a rather sharper curve, and in two hundred yards crossed Enfield Road (Huncoat) by a similar bridge, whence it curved right into the yard of Whinney Hill Brickworks - a smaller works than Nori, and owned by a separate company. Passing through the yard, the line continued parallel to Enfield Road for six hundred yards to Huncoat station. Immediately behind the down platform of the station was situated Huncoat Colliery, where there were extensive sidings and a small engine shed. In 1934, the only extension to this railway was built, a branch line leaving the main route just behind a row of houses (Oak Bank) on Enfield Road, and curving off northwards over the low bulk of Whinney Hill to Moorfield Colliery and the Altham Coke Works, just over a mile away. The site of these establishments is now an industrial estate.

This privately owned railway, with a total length of just under three miles, was controlled from Huncoat Colliery, though the Nori Brickworks section did go its own sweet way to a certain extent. Seven four-wheeled steam tank engines of varying ages served to run the trains, the oldest being built in 1883, and the newest in 1934. *'NORI'* was the property of the Accrington Brick & Tile Company; *'WHINNEY HILL'* was owned by the Whinney Hill Plastic Brick Co., while the other five were the property of George Hargreaves & Co., and operated from Huncoat Colliery, These five were all named after birds - *'ROBIN'*, *'LARK'*, *'LINNET'*, *'KESTREL'*, and *'RAVEN'*. The last two, which were much larger engines, were prohibited on account of their weight from working through to Brick Sidings, and so spent most of their time between Huncoat and Moorfield Collieries. The others could work anywhere on the system, though they rarely worked over Whinney Hill to Altham as they were limited to five loaded wagons over Whinney Hill.

The line was lightly laid, with nothing like the standards of a main line railway, and had many ups and downs as it followed the lie of the land, though except for the Altham branch there were no steep gradients. One or two short embankments were necessary where the line crossed the three bridges - in addition to the two previously mentioned there was another where a small ravine had to be crossed at Oak Bank. These bridges were rather precarious structures, consisting of a double brick wall at each side with two steel girders across the gap to carry the track. In course of time the bridge at the junction became a graveyard for broken wagons; owing to the sharp curve towards Whinney Hill Brickworks there were a number of derailments, and any wagons which fell down the twelve-foot embankment were left to rot away in peace, as recovering them was too difficult. Trains of bricks or coal were worked down to Brick Sidings, to be sorted and await the twice-daily main line engine which came from Accrington to pick them up and take them to Accrington goods yard for onward transmission to their ultimate destinations, the same engine bringing empty wagons for return to the collieries. The resident signalman at Brick Sidings for many years was Bill Caton, an old friend of my family. As a young boy of eight or nine I spent many happy hours in that signal box during school holidays (all very much contrary to regulations!) with Bill. The sidings themselves were controlled by a separate small lever frame in one corner of the box, and as these were small levers, much less than the main line ones, they were quite within my capacity to work them. Consequently I had the time of my life playing with these levers, getting the signals into all sorts of impossible combinations. On at least two occasions a brickworks driver came up into the box in high dudgeon, wanting to know how the so-and-so he was expected to go into three sidings at once, and which of them he was supposed to use. It took all of Bill's diplomacy to get out of these scrapes. On odd occasions a signal inspector would turn up unexpectedly, and in such emergencies I was hurriedly shut into a cupboard till he had gone - much to my disgust. How Bill got away with such breaches of regulations for so long passes my comprehension.

On one occasion when I was in the box with Bill, a brickworks engine (Lark) pushed a rake of wagons into no. 2 siding rather too vigorously, and four of them were derailed, blocking no. 3 siding as well. The Accrington breakdown train had to be summoned, and dealing with the derailed wagons meant that the down main line had to be occupied by the crane, which meant that single line working had to be put in force between Accrington and Huncoat, resulting in considerable delay to main line trains for a few hours. At the subsequent inquiry, it was found that the accident was entirely the fault of the driver. As there was no way I could be found in the signal box with so many official bodies around, Bill smuggled me downstairs into some bushes, where, like Brer Rabbit, I *"lay low and said nuffin"* watching the proceedings. On Saturday afternoons, when there was a cricket match on, around 3.p.m. the brickworks engine - *'NORI'* would creep down the line just past the pavilion, and the crew would climb out onto the saddle tank, where they would sit watching the match for a couple of hours, while the engine simmered gently beneath them. About 5.30 they would climb back into the cab and run back to the works to sign off duty. It was understood that *'NORI'* was always used for this caper as its tank was more comfortable to sit on than those of the smaller engines! It was also whispered (though I took this with a large pinch of salt) that on odd occasions *'NORI'* was specially put in steam for this purpose. The brickworks railway went on its peaceful way through two world wars until the formation of the National Coal Board in 1948. About three years later, things began to disrupt; *'ROBIN'* was transferred to Bank Hall Colliery, Burnley, and shortly afterwards Moorfields Colliery was closed, though the Altham Coke Works remained in use. Gradually the railway fell into disuse, since more and more coal and bricks were transported by road. The brickworks sections continued to function until the late 1950s, when road transport became the norm, and about 1960 the line was closed altogether, the engines being sold for scrap. The track was dismantled and the girders removed from the bridges, leaving only the brick walls, which gradually fell down. Today there are very few vestiges of the line remaining. There is a large expanse of concrete where Huncoat Colliery once stood. The two brickworks are still in business, though their produce goes entirely by road. With the Beeching era beginning in 1964, the main line between Accrington and Huncoat was denuded of all its sidings, and

Brick Sidings signal box was demolished. So passed the Brickworks Railway, after more than seventy years service, and very few people in the town now know that it ever existed. Regrettably, our industrial heritage has largely disappeared with little to show for it. No more will we see (and hear!) *'LARK'* or *'LINNET'* pounding up the rise from Huncoat with a dozen loaded wagons, with the smoke from her chimney going straight up in the air. No more will *'NORI'* creep down the line to watch a cricket match.

MR. TRAM AND TRAIN - ROBERT RUSH

In circles where the history of British tram and train transport is discussed, there is mentioned in revered tones the name of an Accrington chap - Bob Rush. He is nothing short of being an expert.

Born in Lodge Street in 1912, Bob knows exactly when his interest started. He was four years old and living in Burnley Road near the Alice Street stop. An aunt was a tram conductress, and she used to take him for free rides on her tram to Huncoat and Ossie. His interest in railways, especially of the 'Lancashire & Yorkshire' (the L&Y), came later. He wrote about it whilst in the Army during the Second World War. In 1961 his book on Accrington tramways was published. Since then there have been about eight more books, all of which he has illustrated with splendid drawings. Bob could have been a draughtsman if he hadn't chosen pharmacy.

Until de-regulation of 'bus transport in the 1980s, Bob kept notes on the Corporation fleet as he observed them in the streets. Asked for his views on today's trains, he replied, *"I've no interest in diesels - those travelling biscuit tins"*.

'Black 5', no. 45229, steams out of Accrington towards Church in the early 1960s. The rails on the right connected with the Manchester line which had to climb the 'Baxenden Bank', one of Britain's steepest main line railways. *(John Searson)*

120

THE CLAYTON LINE

A letter appeared in the *'Manchester Guardian'* on 9th December 1880 from a writer signing himself *"Clayton-le-Moor"*s, written as if the township were writing. In brief, it bemoaned the fact that *'there are five railway stations within a radius of two miles from here'* but that *'all goods made here need to be carried to Accrington for despatch'.* He implored the Lancashire & Yorkshire Railway Company to construct a line from Accrington to Whalley to connect with the Blackburn to Clitheroe line, saying that he felt like the Ancient Mariner, surrounded by water but not a drop to drink. That company had recently constructed the Great Harwood loop line *'coming from no-whence and leading to no-whither'* but already having developed the district's resources *'as to promise at no distant date to outrun me in the equal race we have hitherto made in the cause of progress'.*

He went on to say that perhaps Whalley viaduct, *'a structure not calculated to give confidence to those who have occasion to travel over it'* might need being taken down and rebuilt, and reminded the editor that a line from Accrington to Chatburn had previously been surveyed but withdrawn due to the opposition of a short-sighted landowner.

A generation later, in 1908, a meeting took place in the Clayton Council Offices, comprised of councillors and local businessmen. They heard a Mr. J. Tertius Wood, a Manchester engineer brought in by the council chairman, J. Riley, tell of his proposals for the use of three lengths of railway, measuring in total 2$^1/_2$ miles. The first was already in existence - that line from Huncoat to the 'Nori' works at Whinney Hill, but it would be extended to Grimshaw Street behind the Conservative Club, near the tram terminus. Another branch line would run from near the quarries on the South side of Burnley Road to Moorfield Pit.

Wood's scheme would involve the closure of Whinney Hill Road and Huncoat Lane. A new road would be constructed from Whalley Road, Altham, to run alongside the railway, meeting Huncoat Lane again at a point near the bottom. This would cost a lot of money. The figure he had in mind was £26,000 which did not include the cost of rolling stock, though it did include the £300 needed for obtaining a legal order. He envisaged being able to raise half the sum outside Clayton. His proposals were enthusiastically received, some even 'getting their hand into their pockets' there and then. The feeling of those present was that the finished scheme would greatly benefit the district.

Wood was not inexperienced in such schemes. He had recently completed one at Clayton, near Barnsley. In concluding, he expressed the opinion that a light railway construction would be cheaper yet suitable, and that he thought the L & Y Railway might run a motor train (a short train with a steam engine built into a carriage and which could be adapted so as to pull and push a set of carriages) from Accrington, similar to one they had recently started on the Bury to Holcombe Brook line.

Why did the scheme not get off the ground? Surely this was thinking along the right lines?

BRIDGE THAT GAP
Les Bond

Enter Accrington from any direction, whether by road, rail or foot, and the massive edifice of the Railway Viaduct is apparent; in some instances from quite a distance. It is on foot, though, that its true magnificence may be properly appreciated.

From the Railway's first appearance in the town in 1848, The Viaduct has stood comfortably astride road and stream, watching over the ever growing community of houses, shops, public houses, schools and the people within them as they flourished and prospered, or just existed and died, round its feet. The Viaduct takes its first modest step where it takes the railway line over Blackburn Road and carries it, gently curving, across 21 arches to deposit it safely at Milnshaw Lane from where it departs for the east of the County and beyond.

Stone corbels - large projections which once supported roof timbers or an upper floor - are still to be seen, clear evidence of the buildings which once occupied the spaces between the supports. These also indicate where the original roads ran, as no corbels were incorporated into the supports which straddled a road. At the time of publication, the only remaining buildings are occupied by a taxi firm and a bathroom accessory shop. Both of these give a clear indication as to how the viaduct may have looked at the turn of the century.

How many children have listened with rapt gullibility to the tale of a military band marching triumphantly into town, along Hyndburn Road, the pipe major flinging and spinning the mace ever higher, until, as they entered the shadow of the Hyndburn Road span, a mighty flick of his huge arm launched the staff spinning and whirling over the top of the Viaduct. Then, without breaking step or altering speed or pace, he led his band out into the sunshine of Bull Bridge and without even the merest upward glance, caught the mace as it plummeted earthwards. I can hear the applause even now. Children can be seen, occasionally, hopelessly attempting to emulate the feat with a stick or brush handle. The structure, now floodlight, is a superb monument to the men who designed and built it. Stand beneath and look up and wonder.

The dominance and fame of the viaduct causes other bridges in the borough to be placed into the background of railway architecture, and this is a pity because they too have their history and interest. You know that the Viaduct is the largest bridge, but which one is the smallest? Where is the lowest? Where do two bridges run parallel, separated by a distance short enough to fit the average car across? Which bridge is built in two halves, one half of iron plates and the other of stone with a brick arch roof?

There may be several claimants to the title of shortest in the (old) borough. The footpath between Within Grove Estate and Huncoat Industrial Estate at just nine feet doesn't get a look in. It is that other well known bridge in the town, that spans the 'Underground' which links Crossland Street and Grant Street and measures a minuscule five feet eight inches that easily takes the crown. The lowest bridge in the town is the concrete construction at the top of Star Street. Approximately six feet high, this bridge covers a path which doesn't go anywhere. At the time of publication the reservoir to which the footpath led has been drained and earth movers are at work.

The Lonsdale Street bridge has been constructed in two separate halves, and it is distinctive in that it is built in two different ways, one half brick and stone, the other half from iron plates riveted together.

Students of architecture or people with an interest in the railway are not the only ones who will find an interest in the heritage left to us by those engineers of long ago. Walk round the town with your eyes open and look at what you see. You just might be amazed.

BEER & THE SPIRIT OF AVIATION

One of the pleasures of looking at the past through old newspapers and in libraries is the joy of meeting a genuine 'character'. A year ago, I met Harry Bergan, who, in the first decade of this departing century, was licensee of the Lang's Arms, a small pub in Grant Street, between Dale Street and the Grammar School. He'd taken over there from his father-in-law and had kept the New Market Tavern in Union Street.

Harry was an engineer at Bullough's before becoming a licensee, though he also had a spell with a touring repertory company, as he had a lot of amateur dramatic experience. He was a member of a local Kentucky Minstrels troupe, and a gifted painter. As a landlord he was regarded as a model in not allowing drunkenness or the spending of wages which hadn't been tipped up to a wife. A good-living man, he supported the newly-opened Ambulance Drill Hall and Sacred Heart Church.

However, Harry's claim to a place in Accrington's Hall of Fame rests on his activities in the world of that newest of sports - aviation. It probably came from his interest in motoring, also still in its infancy. He joined the newly-formed Manchester Aero Club and stated his intention of becoming an aviator, putting his motor car up for sale so that its place in his garage could be taken by an aeroplane. He experimented with a home-built 'plane, had ideas for designs, and had thoughts on the problems of vertical take-off. His publican friends supported Harry, and they proposed, though it never came off, what would have been the country's first air race in an effort to win a £1,000 prize put up by the *'Daily Mail'* for the first one-mile circular flight by an all-British aeroplane. The plan was to fly from Hapton Common to Burnley and Accrington, thus allowing Accy to 'get one up' over Burnley.

A 1909 advert for the Lang's Arms shows Harry's portrait and the wording that he sold ale as well as spare parts for Zeppelin airships. He gave free storage for aeroplanes. However, if he did complete the 'plane he intended to build, he certainly didn't fly it.

Adventure was in Harry's blood. He is reported to have entered a lion's cage when a circus came to town, and in 1917 accepted a lift on the back of a friend's motor cycle combination. On the road from Whitebirk to Rishton, a tyre burst and they collided with a lorry. Harry was killed. Accrington had lost a character who might have been the man to bring the aviation industry to the town, or who might have invented the Harry Jump Jet.

H. Bergan,

LANG'S ARMS

——HOTEL,——

ACCRINGTON.

Thwaites' Mild & Bitter Ales,
Wines & Spirits of the
Best Quality

EVERY courtesy shown to Motorists, and good accommodation, with free storage for Aeroplanes.

All spare parts for Wright Bros. and Count Zeppelin's Airships kept in Stock.

THE ACCRINGTON OBSERVER OBSERVED

Geoffrey Mather

More than half a century ago now, it seemed to me that there was nothing more important in life or on earth than to be a reporter. I had equipped myself as well as I could for this task, acquiring a good shorthand speed and a skill in typewriting to match. I read a lot, but had no other qualification other than desire. I played for Church Cricket Club in the Lancashire League, one of the youngest players of the time because better ones were batting for England on various fields of battle in World War 2. The *'Accrington Observer'* did not always turn up to report extraneous matches - those charity affairs involving trips to Yorkshire, for instance. I did not know anyone at the newspaper, but I filled the gap, unasked, unrewarded, and saw my work in print. I recall particularly one match at Pudsey St. Lawrence (Lancashire v. Yorkshire XI, it said on the posters): I fretted in the pub where the ale was free because I did not have detailed scores. A sub-editor from the *'Lancashire Evening Post'* drove me back to the deserted ground in the darkness to make up the discrepancy. I did not know him. He seems in the memory dark, almost saturnine, a gentleman beyond my reach or class. The memory of youth probably exaggerates. At any rate, my efforts led to my becoming an *'Accrington Observer'* man, licensed to read proofs all week, work at reporting over week-ends, and sell the newspaper to newsagents at 6.30 a.m. on Tuesday mornings. This, for 12s 6d (63p) a week. I would have done it for nothing. The *'Accrington Observer'* was housed in Edgar Street in unpretentious premises and was headed by Mr Richard and Mr Robert S. Crossley. Mr Richard was my boss. He was portly and suffered from indigestion. I had to shop for his indigestion pills. The Editor was a Mr Tom Watson. He could drink up to 40 cups of tea a day and I made them. I made them stronger and stronger until they looked like treacle, but he seemed to enjoy them all the more. In the reporters' room were Roland Joynson, Alan Lambert, Bill Palmer, Frank Kitchener and Cyril Leach. Roland Joynson wore leggings, ate a great deal of peanut butter, and had difficulty with phones, *"What name? Armitage? No. Hewitson? What then? Entwistle? Ah, ah - SMITH!"* How he deranged his hearing to that extent, I will never know, even though phones baffle my own hearing now. Alan Lambert composed music. He was an accomplished pianist and would play Mozart for hours on end. Unsuspecting people would appear and Alan would ask, innocently, *"Care to come to the house for supper?"* If they accepted, he settled them down and Mozarted them to death. Sometimes we lost him. The editor would say, *"Go and find Mr Lambert, will you?"* and I would walk the streets trying to plot where I might find a piano. If I could find a piano, I might find Alan Lambert. There was one in the town hall. When he covered a long-running case in Preston, he wrote his copy returning on the train and it occupied a good half roll of British Rail toilet paper. Bill Palmer had the most manic laugh in creation and he used it to good effect. When amused, he would give every indication of climbing a wall. His joy was very physical. He is said to have organised a cricket match during a works outing. Legend has it that the match was on a hill and the ball kept rolling down the sides. So that when he punted along a river, others on the outing gathered on a bridge to throw clods of earth at him. Perhaps the story is apocryphal: I did not dare ask him. At any rate, he knew his cricket and played it with great concentration and diligence and he taught me much. Frank Kitchener always struck me as being independent of work since I was told he had a shop. He looked prosperous to me. I felt I could never aspire to his status. Cyril Leach was a mystery. He had arrived from the big newspapers in Manchester and could carry on a conversation about economics while typing a report at great speed concerning council housing. He was highly political, of the Leftwards persuasion, and I used to read his carbon paper to see what he had been up to. Once, at a cricket match, he lectured me for an hour on a book called *'The Germans'*, by, I think, Emil Ludwig. That was more his style than cricket. A doctor appeared regularly in the reporters' room at the time. I forget his name, but he had a foreign intonation, and he put forward the theory that at the end of the war all Germans between the ages of 16 and 65 should be castrated. It is only now that I know what castration means that I realise the enormity of the proposition. But he was serious. Dick Pearson was a reporter who had preceded me. His name was a legend. He had a temper. On Friday nights people played cards in the proof reader's office. If Dick was losing, he was apt to gather up the cards, march downstairs, and post them down the nearest drain. He once played golf with his editor. Frustrated by the game, he broke his club over his knee and marched off shouting, *"If you want that meeting covered on Sunday night, cover it your bloody self."* On Saturday mornings the reporters tended to chat in their room and they were joined by Joe Higgin, the *'Lancashire Evening Post's'* man. Joe was eccentric, highly intelligent, and well regarded. He had worked in London for Press Association, tended to use a bicycle as his form of locomotion and had all the appearances of a solicitor in his dark clothing had it not been for the hole in his sock. I never saw a Mrs. Higgin, so I assume he was a bachelor. He liked geraniums and bought some from a man who knocked on his door at night. The following morning, he discovered they were his own geraniums, plucked from his garden. When the town centre was jammed by cars because firemen were trying to rescue a cat from a high viaduct he declined to attend saying, *"I have five cats at home, and nobody gives a damn about them except me."* He spent time at the steps leading to the town centre lavatories and his explanation was simple: *"Anybody you wish to see ends up there at one time or another."* Conversations on Saturdays were erudite: Lenin, Victoria, Elizabeth I, philosophy, economics, all were dissected. I went to work on Saturday mornings to be educated. My presence was not requested. I attended for the joy of it. Never, it seemed to me then, was there such a learned bench of elders. So I played my cricket on Saturdays and learned my trade. On Monday mornings, I would be brimming with information about Saturday's game, and the sequence was invariably the same. I would join Guy Cunliffe, the reader, or proof-checker, in his small office with its bare floor boards. And he would say, *"Good game, was it? I remember Charlie Llewellyn..."* Llewellyn had played for Accrington. Guy remembered games from before I was born and I was never able to describe mine. I am possibly the only Lancashire League player who ran up and down main roads in whites while games were in progress, my studs clacking on the pavements. This is because a Blackburn *'Telegraph'* reporter named Dennis Ditchfield paid me 2s 6d (13p) per game to phone reports at hourly intervals to his office. The phone was in the centre of West End, Oswaldtwistle. Hence my frequent trips. At the other end was a telephonist named Cissie Fine. I would begin my hysterical babble and she would say, *"Calm down, calm down. It's all right. There's no rush"* like a psychiatrist dealing with a particularly deranged patient. Eventually I moved to the *'Evening Telegraph'* myself, for £1 a week, and Mr Richard Crossley said I was not ready for the "big-time." He could have been right. But I spent 12 years on the *'Telegraph'* and 30 at the *'Daily Express'*. And sometimes, now, I look at the *'Observer's'* old place in Edgar Street and fancy I smell the oily machinery and hear the thud of feet on bare boards. I see the urgent faces of my elders and betters, and hear the joyful laugh of Bill Palmer, for the essence of them all is either still there or my memory makes it so. They wrote long, accurate reports and had good shorthand, and these qualities are in short supply today. *'The Observer'*, I note, is no longer anonymous in its side street, but flaunts itself on the main road. I hope it was ready for the big time.

OAK HILL AND ALICE

Josie Green

Sunday 2ⁿᵈ April 1995 was a lovely day in Accrington. After a week of rain, wind and snow, Spring had arrived. In Oak Hill Park a group of people gathered outside the old Mansion House in the sunshine; a large group of over a hundred smiling men and women - and a White Rabbit.

When Thomas Hargreaves built Oak Hill in 1815 as a home for his family, the new house reflected the prosperity of the calico-printing firm of Hargreaves & Dugdale of Broad Oak. After Thomas died in 1822, aged only fifty, the business continued to thrive, his own partnership having been taken over by his eldest son John. His widow Nancy, his second wife, continued to live at Oak Hill with the younger children, and as his sons became old enough, several of them entered the works and became partners. They also built their own homes in the growing town; John built the original Broad Oak House; Benjamin built Arden Hall; and Robert lived at Bank House. In 1840, the youngest son came of age and under the terms of his father's will, the estate could finally be settled. Jonathan Hargreaves, the fourth surviving son, became the new owner of Oak Hill, to which he later added a new wing. The firm, now Hargreaves Bros. & Co., and the family continued to prosper, as did Accrington Itself, benefitting from their success.

The 1851 Census shows Jonathan living at Oak Hill with his wife, Anna Maria, and their two small daughters, and a household staff of seven. On 13ᵗʰ October 1852, their only surviving son, Reginald Gervis Hargreaves, was born. The Census also reveals a workforce of eight hundred and seventy-six employees at Broad Oak; but soon there were big changes. By 1854, only Jonathan was left to run the firm, and he decided the best way to keep the business going would be to let it pass into other hands. In 1856 it was taken over by F. W. Grafton & Co. and went on to enjoy remarkable success.

Soon after Grafton took over at Broad Oak, Jonathan Hargreaves and his family left Accrington to live in Hampshire where he bought an estate called Cuffnells near Lyndhurst. There, Jonathan lived the life of a farmer, landowner and Justice of the Peace. He never returned to live in Oak Hill, as he had hoped; he died in 1863, aged fifty-two, less than seven years after moving away. Like his father, he left a widow and young family. By his will, the residue of his estate was left to his only son, Reginald, on his reaching the age of twenty-five. Reginald Gervis Hargreaves was educated at Eton, and in 1872 entered Christ Church, Oxford University, as an undergraduate.

From 1855 to 1891, the Dean of Christ Church was a clergyman called Henry George Liddell. He was a great scholar, and the father of a little girl called Alice. Among the staff at Christ Church was Rev. Charles Lutwidge Dodgson. He was a Lecturer in mathematics and spent his working life in Oxford where Reginald Hargreaves was one of his students. The new art of photography was sweeping England in the 1850s, and Dodgson became one of its most enthusiastic exponents. He has been acclaimed as the most outstanding photographer of children in the nineteenth century. Among his favourite subjects were the children of the Dean, and particularly his daughter, Alice. In July 1862, he and a colleague at Oxford took the three Liddell girls, Lorina, Alice and Edith, for a trip on the river, and during this journey he made up a story to amuse them. They enjoyed it so much that afterwards Alice, then aged ten, begged him to write it down for her. In 1865, Alice's story was published, under Dodgson's pen name, *'Lewis Carroll'*, as *'Alice in Wonderland'*.

Reginald Hargreaves was a student at Christ Church between 1872 and 1878, and during this time he became acquainted with the Liddell sisters. In his last year at Oxford he reached the age of twenty-five, and became the owner of Cuffnells and Oak Hill. On 15th September 1880, Reginald Gervis Hargreaves and Alice Pleasance Liddell were married in Westminster Abbey.

Reginald and Alice Hargreaves had three sons, who were all baptised by the Rev. Charles Dodgson in Lyndhurst Church. Two of their sons died during service in the 1914-1918 War. The third son was Caryl Liddell Hargreaves, who survived, and his daughter Mrs. Mary Jean Rosalie St. Clair, of Tetbury, Gloucs., is their only grandchild. Reginald Hargreaves died in 1926, and his wife in 1934; they are buried at Lyndhurst, as are Reginald's parents.

Meanwhile, in Accrington, the Oak Hill estate was neglected. The house was tenanted from the time Jonathan Hargreaves left in 1856 until about 1880, but since then had been empty. In July 1888, Mrs. Reginald Hargreaves visited Accrington with her husband for the first time to lay one of the foundation stones of the Benjamin Hargreaves School, where she was warmly welcomed by a huge crowd. In 1890 Reginald was approached by Accrington Council who wished to purchase the land to create a park. After negotiations, Accrington bought the estate for approximately £12,000. The neglected grounds were landscaped and laid out as a park, Reginald Hargreaves performed the Opening Ceremony on Whit Monday, 22nd May 1893, amid crowds of enthusiastic people.

The house was renovated and opened as a museum in 1900, but was never to enjoy the care and attention lavished on the Park. Its contents consisted almost entirely of donated items. The Museum was closed *'for the duration of hostilities'* at the beginning of the Second World War, but in fact was never reopened. It was finally closed and its contents dispersed in the early 1950s.

After the closure, Oak Hill was used for a number of temporary purposes. From 1952, when dry rot was discovered, the condition of the building continued to deteriorate, and from 1964 there was pressure for it to be demolished. It survived by default rather than intent through the intervention of public expenditure cuts and then the reorganisation of Local Government in 1974. By 1976 it was *'one of the saddest sights in Hyndburn'*.

It took almost twenty years for that description to be revised. In those years many people and organisations, local and national, were united in their efforts to save Oak Hill. However, it was not until 1993, when the key and ownership of the building was formerly handed over to the Abbeyfield Hyndburn Society Ltd. for one shining £1 coin, that its future was assured. What followed was a complete transformation, as the building contractors demolished Jonathan Hargreaves' 1850s extension, gutted the interior, replaced the roof and created a beautiful home for twelve elderly people. Viewed from the slopes of the park, Oak Hill is now a beautiful sight, looking as it must have done when Thomas Hargreaves built it.

The people standing in the sunshine on 2nd April were some of those who had fought to save Oak Hill, representatives of the organisations involved, the Abbeyfield Society who now owned it, and some of the residents. Reginald and Alice's grand-daughter, Mrs. St. Clair, performed the official Opening Ceremony. The White Rabbit? - he came to remind us all of the link between the real Alice, Lewis Carroll's *'Dream Child'* and the Hargreaves family.

ANYONE FOR TENNIS?

Helen Barrett

Did you know of the connection between Wimbledon and Accrington? More precisely, its a link between Accrington Cemetery, the Church of St. John the Evangelist, the old Wesley Methodist Church on Abbey Street, and the All-England Tennis Club.

What all these buildings have in common is the name Macaulay. St. John's Church, the Cemetery and the Wesley Church were all designed by the architect Henry Macaulay. Henry was a native of Huddersfield and came to Accrington soon after his marriage to Mary Lightfoot at Christ Church in December 1859. Mary was the daughter of Thomas Lightfoot, a brother of John Emmanuel Lightfoot, later the first Mayor of Accrington.

Henry and Mary lived at 86 Manchester Road, and Henry's architectural practice was situated at 91 Blackburn Road. Six children were born to Henry and Mary, four of them born before they left Accrington about 1870. Archibald, their only son, was born in 1867 and baptised at Christ Church.

In 1876, Henry was appointed Borough Surveyor of Kingston-upon-Thames. He held this post for over thirty years. Henry's son, Archibald, married Amy Lloyd, a notable Kent sportswoman, and no doubt her influence on their son, Duncan, was of paramount importance.

Duncan Macaulay began to play tennis at the age of ten, and as both his parents were keen on the game, he was taken to watch tournaments at a very early age. Leaving school, Duncan joined the Army, and after the end of the 1914-1918 War, he transferred to the Indian Army. In India, Duncan took every opportunity he could to improve his game. Back in England on leave in 1922 he played in all the tournaments leading up to Wimbledon. Failing to be accepted for the championships, he applied to be taken on as an umpire, and so it was in that capacity that he first appeared officially at Wimbledon. This was the beginning of a long association with the All-England Club.

Later Duncan became a referee at a variety of tournaments and in 1937 he was appointed Assistant Referee at Wimbledon, a post he held until the outbreak of war. During the war the championships were abandoned. Towards the end of the War, Duncan ran a tennis event at Aldershot in aid of the Red Cross. A lot of pre-war Wimbledon players were roped in, including Mme. Mathieu, who was then serving with the Free French Forces in Britain. During the early part of 1945 the American Forces in Britain held their championships at Wimbledon, and Duncan was allowed, by the War Office, to act as referee.

As hostilities ceased, moves began to be made to re-establish the Wimbledon Championships. In January 1946, Duncan was appointed Secretary to the All-English Club. The immediate post-war years were very difficult for the club and Duncan played a prominent role in reorganizing and revitalizing its administration. But for the job Duncan did in that austere period, Wimbledon could not have retained its status as a major championship ground.

For seventeen years, Duncan served as Secretary and his name came to be known by tennis players throughout the world. In May 1963 Duncan retired although he still captained the British Davis Cup Team in 1963 and 1964. In retirement in 1965 he wrote the book *'Behind the scenes at Wimbledon'*, an account of his experiences, and a history of the Club.

At the age of 85 in October 1982 Duncan died. A bachelor, the Macaulay line died with him. Duncan was a remarkable personality in British tennis for almost forty years, and it is due to his business acumen and far-sightedness that the present-day championships are what they are.

So if you're like me and the Wimbledon fortnight means two weeks of being '*glued to the box*', pause and remember Duncan, the son of an Accrington man. Next time you're on the top of The Coppice, look at Accrington's sky-line and consider the contribution Duncan's grandfather Henry made to the townscape by designing St. John's Church. Grandfather and grandson's achievements have both stood the test of time.

THE SNOW'S ON PENDLE HILL

Benita Moore

Most people think of Lancashire
As 'County of the poor',
They do not see the green, green hills
And purple heathered moor.
Yet I see only beauty
Not the dark, satanic mill,
When the sky is flushed with sunrise
And the snow's on Pendle Hill.

If you want to find contentment
Simply walk the Pendle way,
Up from Downham into Barley
Where the bright streams gently play
And the April rainbows shimmer
Round the hawthorn's new green frill,
Sweet contentment thronging through you
When the snow's on Pendle Hill.

When the tawny owls glitter
On a flurry of moonbeams
And the rainbowed stars pierce fiercely
Through the curtain of your dreams.
Witches' voices taunt and tingle
When cold winter's breath is still
And the ghosts of ages linger
When the snow's on Pendle Hill.

You can nestle in your cottage
Where the coal fires swiftly burn
And the gentle hiss of kettle
With the ticking clock will gurn,
When the storms outside rage fiercely
Yet your cosy haven's still,
With the whitewashed walls withstanding
Like the snow's on Pendle Hill.

Oh, I do not crave for power
Nor for fortune or for fame,
For as a wise man uttered:
'Sure there's nothing in a name'.
Yes, all I ask is peace of mind,
A bright robin on the sill
With a loved one close besides me
When the snow's on Pendle Hill.

LOCAL LIMERICKS

John Sephton

A 'oming-pigeon fancier from Accrington
'Ad a white-ringt cropped pigeon and a black-ringt un,
Cropped brid 'ad to walk,
So 'e learned it to talk,
'An ask folks t' best road back to Accrington.

Lass wi' uncle an' aunty in Antley
Said, 'Ah don't reck'n me aunt's very auntly;
Me uncle's reet uncly,
Though bein' so carbuncly
'E just can't sit down theer in Antley'.

There were a young feller fro' Baxenden,
Who'd a Mercerised new shirt an' a Jacksoned un;
'E said 'Mercerised un's nice,
It's a bit 'igher price,
But Jacksoned 'un won't do fer Baxenden'.

A bride wi' no groom at Church church
Sniffed, 'Reckon Ah've bin left i' t'lurch,
'E's nobbut a lad lad,
Not really bad bad,
But 'e wants knockin' off 'is purch purch!'

A dressy owd jigger fro' Huncoyt
Bowt a gun-dog, gun-cap and a gun-coyt;
Dog's foot caught i' t'trigger,
It missed the owd jigger,
But peppered 'is cap an' 'is gun-coyt.

When a scruffy young lass fro' Wood Nook
Come past, folks theer all 'ad a good look;
They could see some rare scenes
Through the 'oles in 'er jeans,
But said, 'Ne'er mind, oo's appen a good cook'.

NOTCHEL CRYING

In Frank Hird's book *'Lancashire Stories'*, he tells that *'as late as 1859 the custom of notchel crying was observed at Accrington'*. This was a means by which a husband would employ a bellman to publicly proclaim that he will no longer be responsible for any debts incurred by his wife. In March that year, the bellman was so employed. However, later the same day, he was engaged by the wife to announce that she would not be responsible for his debts, that she had doubts about his fidelity, and that if he had given her more housekeeping instead of spending it on other women, they could have lived in comfort. 'Great crowds followed the bellman through the streets'.

In September 1926, Crossley and Ainsworth wrote in the *'Accrington Observer'* of this *'former practice'*, which resulted in a letter to them from *'One interested'* to say that he *'had observed the practice in one of the townships of greater Accrington about 5.30 pm in March or April 1923'*.

Is there scope for someone to set up a new business along these lines?

GRANDMA ON THE GARDEN PATH

Catherine Duckworth

Scattered through this book, as with many others, are photographs old and new. The better books tell you where the photograph has come from, whether from private individuals or a collection, many of which are in local libraries. At Accrington Local Studies Library, the town is fortunate in having a large collection of photographs going back many years and covering a wide variety of subjects. They are used in many different books and pamphlets world wide.

What sort of photographs do we have? Well, the majority of our collection is black and white because they last indefinitely, but we also have box brownie type snaps, glass slides and negatives and some enlargements. Few are the size of the photo of the Accrington Pals on the wall in the Local Studies library. This was used as a backcloth at the Octagon Theatre, Bolton, for the production of Peter Whelan's play 'The Accrington Pals'. We also have the William Turner collection of photographs he gathered together whilst researching his two books on the Accrington Pals.

What other subjects do we cover? We try to cover everything from the earliest date up to the present. Our largest coverage is for Accrington as it is only since 1974 that the townships of Hyndburn have come officially into our remit. However, the Accrington and District Historical Association members were people of vision, and their photos cover all our area. They made an effort to record every old building in the area so have recorded many that are now long gone.

We have aerial photographs, photographs of royal visits, stone layings, walking days, funerals, fires and floods, street scenes, market stalls, churches, beauty spots… and the not so beautiful!

So if you're thinking of throwing out your snapshots, think again! That view of Grandma walking up her garden path might just have the only known photograph of a tripe seller in the background.

WILLIAM & ANNE HAWORTH AND 'HOLLINS HILL'

Jennifer Rennie

Visitors to the Haworth Art Gallery are often surprised at its intimate atmosphere and charming decorative details. Far from the institutional feeling at most local authority-owned buildings, The Haworth still speaks eloquently of the personalities, interests and concerns of the original owners, William and Anne Haworth.

William (1849-1913) and his sister Anne (1845-1920) were the only children of Thomas Haworth, one of the most successful cotton manufacturers in Accrington in the latter part of the 19th century. They were leading members of the Cannon Street Baptist Church, and ardent music lovers. They had lived in the family house, Windsor Place in Burnley Road, for many years when William decided to embark on the building of another home where he and his sister could pass their later years. He was already in his sixties, and Anne was unwell enough to have to spend periods of up to six weeks in bed. No doubt William thought of this when he bought the farmland on the hills south of Accrington where Hollins Hill was to be built; Anne's bedroom has superb views which she must have been able to see from her bed.

The Haworths secured the services of a Yorkshire architect, Walter Brierley, to build their Tudor-style home with symmetrical two-storey bay windows, a medieval-style entrance hall and staircase with massive leaded window. The porch was designed to be surmounted by eleven heraldic animals. The inside was decorated with carved details of animals, birds and foliage. Elaborate stucco ceilings were designed for two of the reception rooms, and the spacious grounds, with outbuildings, stable block and coachman's cottage, were

Joseph Taylor at the wheel of the family's Rolls-Royce Silver Ghost, a green 'Double Laudaulette' model, purchased in 1912. It was sold in 1921 to Lady Macalpine.

landscaped with rhododendrons and a rose garden. Hollins Hill was completed towards the end of 1909.

It is obvious from the decorative details of Hollins Hill that William and Anne loved animals and birds. Their preference is echoed in their choice of pictures for their home. One particular favourite with visitors is *'My Ladye's Palfrey'* by J.F.Herring, which features a medieval scene with lady and gentleman in elaborate costume, with two horses, one black, one grey. The Haworths loved horses and Anne reverted to horse and carriage when the chauffeur left for the Great War. Their pictures show their liking for somewhat idealised views of everyday life and events. All but a few landscape and seascape subjects including animals or children.

There is little evidence available to cast light on daily life at Hollins Hill. We know that William had many public duties to perform as well as running the firm, *'Thomas Haworth & Son'*. He was a member of the Liberal Club, President of the Mechanics' Institute, a County Councillor and a magistrate. He was also President of the Accrington Choral Society and the Amateur Dramatic Society.

Anne's time was also taken up with public duties and she was a fervent supporter of Accrington Victoria Hospital. They provided the hospital's first motorised ambulance in 1915. She also helped organise the knitting of comforts to send to soldiers in the Great War. Most of her time would have been taken up with the running of Hollins Hill and its staff, which she achieved with the help of her companion, Miss Priestley.

Lucy Ratcliffe remembers the Haworths and many of those who worked for them at Hollins Hill between 1910 and 1920. Her father, Joseph Taylor, was the Haworths' chauffeur from 1907 and he took them away on holiday for six weeks each year, usually to Scotland. During this time, the house was cleaned from top to toe. This was an opportunity for the children of the staff to explore rooms they were usually not allowed to enter. She remembers Bessie Stanley, the 'general help', and Mrs. MacDonald who came in to help with the laundry. There was Mr. Whiston, the butler, and Mr. Beech, the coachman. Lucy was a regular visitor to Anne during the war. She would be shown in by Lucy Egerton, the maid, who was 'so small she only came half-away up the door'. Anne was always reclining on a sofa in the dining room, and Lucy would talk to her for up to an hour at a time. She sometimes took Anne freshly-laid eggs from her mother's hens. Her mother sent her with a bunch of sweet peas when news of Anne's death reached the neighbourhood.

Considering that Hollins Hill was designed with no less than five guest bedrooms, it is surprising that the Haworths rarely had people to stay. One exception to this was Joseph Briggs, who was later to give Accrington its internationally-famous collection of Tiffany glass. He was a school friend of William's, though he had spent most of his adult life working in the Tiffany Studios in New York. It is tempting to speculate that the idea of Joseph sending a collection of Tiffany glass back to Accrington was born as the two men discussed the importance of the town having an art gallery and collections to display in it.

William died in 1913, and it is said that Anne never recovered from his loss. She continued to buy paintings and eventually bequeathed fifty of them, along with Hollins Hill, its grounds and buildings, to the town which has secured the wealth of the Haworth family. In doing this, she achieved her brother's aim to provide an Art Gallery for Accrington people.

DID YOU KNOW?

That a novel, 'The Man in the Iron Mask' (based on that of the same name by Dumas), written by Peter Hoyle (pub. 1986 Carnacet) and set in 'run-down provincial Northern England' has Accrington connections? Peter attended St. John's School and the Grammar School in the 1950s before becoming a librarian. The opening page describes an advertising slogan on a building - *'Half the Male Population of this District is wearing Cash & Co.'s hats'*. Could Peter have remembered that Cash & Co. had their shop at the corner of Peel Street and Blackburn Road, opposite the Commercial Hotel, when he was a lad? Could he have seen their name sign? It was so big he couldn't have missed it. ✽✽✽✽✽✽✽ That in 1913, a Mr. Slater of Avenue Parade, fixed a 40 foot pole through the roof of his house and from it suspended some aerial wires *'which serve to intercept the electric waves'*? This was the first wireless telegraphy apparatus to receive commercial messages in Accrington. ✽✽✽✽✽✽✽ That a Mayor of Accrington officiated as linesman in the F.A. Cup Final in 1910? Dick Watson was Mayor from 1928 to 1930 and he died whilst serving. He had been a keen footballer and administrator. He became a director of the Stanley, a temperance worker and *'did much to cultivate a healthy spirit and higher moral tone amongst footballers'*. ✽✽✽✽✽✽✽ That Mary Ann Street, built where now the Inland Revenue offices are, behind the Castle Hotel, had its name changed through the persistence of three-quarters of the residents wanting to change to the 'classier' name of Milton Street in 1930. The street had originally been named after one of Jonathan Peel's 9 children. The Peel's lived in Accrington House, so their child's name should not have been looked down upon. Some of their other children's names are still enshrined in local streets:- Alice, Robert, William and Spencer. ✽✽✽✽✽✽✽ That Thwaites Road, Ossie, was built on a piece of land owned by the Thwaites brewers. There already was a short piece of road called by that name, opposite the Hare and Hounds pub, when in 1915 the local U.D.C. agreed with the brewing family to construct a road 2,829 feet long and 45 feet wide at a cost of £6,521. The brewers re-paid £3,407 of this. The road ran through their Falls, Fountains and Stanhill Farms. ✽✽✽✽✽✽✽ That in Christ Church graveyard lies John Walmesley, formerly of Baxenden, who died in 1863 aged 42 years. He invented the double shuttle loom and was the principal inventor of a machine called *'The Slasher'*. ✽✽✽✽✽✽✽ That Accrington, although spelled differently, was first mentioned in a document dated 1194 when King Richard 'the Lion Heart' ruled. The township was first mentioned in an Act of Parliament in 1609. The Act related to the ownership of land around Clitheroe. Both Ekwall and Sephton, the top authorities on place names, say that the name is derived from an old English personal name. However, Ekwall does say that the name could mean *'Acorn town'* and we known that the area was forested. *'Oak mast'* was of great importance as a food for swine, and a hamlet may well have been named after that produce. ✽✽✽✽✽✽✽ That Accrington's first 'bus Inspectress was appointed in May 1944. Miss Laura Turner of Midland Street was also expected to look after the welfare of the other 'clippies', as the conductresses were called. The war had put women into what had traditionally been seen as jobs for men. ✽✽✽✽✽✽✽ That, when the Accrington Corporation Steam Tramways Company Limited was formed in 1885, there were no local shareholders. George Alldred, the main contractor, had 15 shares, the rest were taken up by men with ten each:- Charles Courtney Cramp, William Alfred Cubitt, Kenneth McDowie, Alfred Love, Frederick Goulding, Nathan Claydon, Richard Stevens, Walter Stevens, all of whom lived in London, and William Penrose Green, a Leeds engineer. ❋❋❋❋❋❋ That, in 1909, Walter Yearsley and Theodore E. Birch wrote and published *'A Practical Self-Cure of Stammering and Stuttering'* from their address *'The Auto-Phonetic Academy and School for Stammerers'*, at 59 Avenue Parade. Yearsley was a 'speech specialist', Birch was 'an electric light and pure engineer, specialising in electric plating, polishing and lacquering' from his workshop at 135b Blackburn Road. He lived at 414 Blackburn Road. ❋❋❋❋❋❋ That in April 1925, the whole of the choir of St. James', Church Kirk, 'walked out' after a quarrel with the vicar. Thirty members of the congregation went with them. ❋❋❋❋❋❋ In the 1850s, Accrington folk had a choice of six places in the township where they could be buried. There was a strong wish that the town itself should have a burial ground. The strongest voice calling for this was William Barnes, a wealthy manufacturer who lived in the most prestigious address - Accrington House. Under his guidance, the Guardians bought 26 acres of land in Huncoat, off Burnley Road, built a chapel on it and opened for business. The very first person to be buried there was William Barnes, who died 7th October 1864 of chronic hepatitis, aged 48 years, and became entry No.1 in the first Burials Register. He occupies grave plot 19 in the area marked for Dissenters. On the first page of that Burials Book are 20 names. Four of them are Barnes' from different addresses. Two others are Pollard children from 138 Blackburn Road, who died two weeks apart. In the first year from William Barnes' interment there were 65 burials. In 1994 there were 139, and 991 cremations, bringing the total of burials to 58,897. Cremations started in September 1956 and by the last day of 1994 there had been 34,647. ❋❋❋❋❋❋ That after the Second World War, there was a nationwide feeling towards the building of affordable, rented housing. In 1946, the Corporation contracted with Leonard Frankland Ltd. to build 40 three-bedroom houses, 'Hollins Estate', on the Hollins Farm at the top of Royds Street, for £45,809 (£1,145 each) and with Laing's to build 128 houses on the 'Fern Gore' and 'Richmond Hill' estates for £140,323 (£1096 each). These latter were called 'Easiform' houses. ❋❋❋❋❋❋ That in the following year, the Corporation bought six 33-seater single decker 'Arab' buses from Guy Motors for £3,187 each and a Refuse Collector Vehicle for £925 from Dennis Motors. ❋❋❋❋❋❋ That Samson once visited Accrington? There's no written record of it, but who else could have lifted into position the ENORMOUS flagstone, measuring 8 feet 1 inch by 13 feet 10 inches overall which lies between the wall and the front door of Whalley Road United Reform (Congregational) Church? This monolithic slab could lay claim to being the biggest piece of stone in the country, perhaps in the world. To measure its thickness would prove difficult, but assuming it is 2 inches thick (and it is certainly thicker, as a flag of such proportions and thickness would likely snap) then it is estimated by a stone specialist to weigh one ton. At 4 inches it would weigh double. Samson or Hercules, whoever put it down did so when the church was put up in 1876. Men who would know were the site mason, Thompson Westwell, and the clerk of works, Eli Knowles. ❋❋❋❋❋❋ That, although the GPO's 'List of Telephone Subscribers to the Telephone Exchange System' shows '1' as the number of the Manchester Evening News at 131b Blackburn Road, a report in the *'Accrington Observer'* in January 1880, (19 years later) states that the first local telephone had just been installed by a Manchester Company in the works of Benjamin Wilkinson of Ossie. He had chemical works at White Ash and another at Brookside. Installation to allow for communication between these two points a quarter of a mile apart took one week. *'The acoustic properties are very distinct'*. Lines were carried on poles over the fields. By the

1890s, the National Telephone Company had offices at 30 St. James Street and had 58 local installations, The Post Office took over all private systems in 1911. ✸✸✸✸✸✸ That the present fish market was opened in 1961 at a cost of £14,595. It replaced one used since 1870. ✸✸✸✸✸✸ That a song, 'Accrington Pals', written by Mike Harding, appears in his book 'Bombers' Moon', published in 1987. ✸✸✸✸✸✸ That a play, 'Accrington Pals', written by Peter Whelan, was first produced by the Royal Shakespeare Company, who had commissioned it, in 1981, since when it has become popular throughout the country. ✸✸✸✸✸✸ That William Shakespeare performed in Accrington. Don't jump to conclusions - this wasn't the Bard of Stratford on Avon, but a chap of that name who came to play at a concert held in 1869 to mark the opening of the new Market Hall, and he played the piano, or, as a journalist covering the event said, 'he executed Rigoletto on the pianoforte'. ✸✸✸✸✸✸ That Saturday morning pictures, a weekly release into Fantasyland for a generation of Accrington children, started in 1944 when an additional licences was granted to permit the formation of the 'Odeon Cinema Club'. Reporting on it, the Chief Constable said soon afterwards that '1800 children have joined and most attend each Saturday morning to hear addresses and see specially chosen films. It is a non-profitmaking concern with very commendable objects'. Let's hear you all singing: 'We come along on Saturday morning, greeting everybody with a smile. We come along on Saturday morning, knowing it's worthwhile. As members of the Odeon Club, we all intend to be good citizens when we grow up, and champions of the free......'